Praise for

BUDDING LOTUS IN THE WEST

"Finally! Nhi Yến Đỗ Trần has peeled back the layers of mysticism and misogyny that have obscured Buddhism—and its foundational tenets of love and inclusion—for far too long. This book may horrify the gatekeepers, but I suspect the Buddha is smiling."

—Norea K. Hoeft

"*Budding Lotus in the West* is an essential, thought-provoking addition to Buddhist literature. It provides a deep dive into the Buddha's teachings, blending them with engaging stories of his disciples and Nhi's insightful, occasionally hilarious personal anecdotes. Equally instructive and entertaining, it addresses modern issues like abortion, marriage equality, and racism. This book is needed for our world, and everyone—Buddhist or not—would benefit from reading and reflecting on its many helpful and timely lessons."

—Vu Le, creator of NonprofitAF.com and founding board member of Community-Centric Fundraising

"Nhi Yến Đỗ Trần gives us a precious gift: clarity that is born of her deep spiritual practice, scholarship, and humanity. She reveals a spirituality in its purest form—stripped of the same toxic additives that the Buddha rejected. Nhi welcomes us into her own uneasy journey toward enlightenment and compels us to see clearly by removing our egos—the egos that have, over centuries, extinguished many aspects of the female form. Whether you are curious about Buddhism or a devout follower, this book will motivate your desire to seek truth in everything."

—**Inger Piena Brinck**, staff to President Bill Clinton's Advisory Council on Ending Violence Against Women; speaker at World Bank Women's Peace Conference; former cabinet member of Washington governor Jay Inslee

"In this powerful and timely collection of insights, Nhi Yến Đỗ Trần examines centuries of Buddhist doctrine through a contemporary feminist lens. With intelligence, compassion, and wry wit, she interprets the Buddha's teachings as they relate to current issues such as abortion, gun rights, and gender equality. Nhi combines scholarly analysis with personal experience and a dash of skepticism, handling her topics with both the firm hand they warrant and a light touch that makes for compelling and approachable reading. What results is an engaging and refreshing perspective on Buddhist philosophy for committed followers and fresh and intriguing insights for the curious."

—**Lisa Manterfield**, author of *All Our Lies Are True*

"*Budding Lotus in the West* offers a timely look at modern issues and concerns in light of traditional Buddhism, illuminating Buddhism from a personal and cultural perspective. Nhi intertwines her personal story of being raised in a traditional Buddhist family with a necessary new understanding of ancient Buddhist texts and teachings."

—**Eileen Kiera**, Dharma teacher and founder of Mountain Lamp Community

"Regardless of your familiarity with Buddhism, *Budding Lotus in the West* brims with smart insights and a nuanced analysis of a globally revered religion. In our polarized world, Nhi's perspective is a breath of fresh air—firm yet kind, imbued with the heartfelt sincerity of a dedicated Buddhist. Beyond its depth, her personal narrative is endearing, relatable, and delightfully witty."

—**Julie Pham**, PhD, creator of the 7 Forms of Respect; CEO of CuriosityBased.com; co-owner of *Northwest Vietnamese News*

"A captivating, engaging, and insightful journey—I couldn't put it down and find myself eager to share it with my Buddhist friends. Nhi's rich experience and personal accounts add a unique dimension, bridging traditional Buddhist practice with the contemporary American context. Her approach of treating ancient wisdom as hypotheses to be validated through individual experiences offers a refreshing perspective. *Budding Lotus in the West* is an invaluable guide for anyone navigating the complexities of modern spirituality."

—**Jeremy Sherman**, member of Cherry Blossom Sangha and former Buddhist monastic aspirant

"A reckoning on the hypocrisy and sexism in Buddhist organizations. With candor and wit, Nhi offers brave insight and practical solutions while exposing the underbelly of this beloved tradition."

—**Susan Lieu**, author of *The Manicurist's Daughter*

"*Budding Lotus in the West* is a gentle yet firm reminder of women's equal place in Buddhism and life. Women have been integral to religious traditions since time immemorial, yet their contributions have often been overlooked. Following the actionable steps and practical ideas outlined in this book paves the way for us to collectively redress this historical under-recognition and under-appreciation."

—**Erin Okuno**, creator of Fakequity.com and principal at Okuno Consulting

"Nhi Yến Đỗ Trần's writing exhibits a deep courage—both in her critical examination of the contradictions within Buddhist philosophy across all major lineages, and in sharing her complex, personal journey on the path to liberation. Western Buddhist communities stand to gain much from Nhi's insights."

—**Nathan Bombardier**, Cherry Blossom Sangha co-facilitator

"A bow of gratitude to Nhi Yến Đỗ Trần for her insightful critique of Buddhism in the West. Interweaving her own compelling story as a Vietnamese immigrant and feminist trying to find a place within Buddhist tradition with historical scholarship and light touches of humor, Nhi shines a steady light on the sexism that often infuses practice communities. While acknowledging teachers like venerable Zen master Thích Nhất Hạnh for creating a more inclusive sangha, Nhi invites Buddhist practitioners everywhere to embrace a compassionate, socially just community of practice for the benefit of all beings and the earth."

—**Holly J. Hughes**, author of *The Pen and the Bell: Mindful Writing in a Busy World*

Budding Lotus in the West

Budding Lotus in the West

Buddhism *from an* Immigrant's Feminist Perspective

NHI YẾN ĐỖ TRẦN

Broadleaf Books
Minneapolis

BUDDING LOTUS IN THE WEST
Buddhism from an Immigrant's Feminist Perspective

29 28 27 26 25 24 1 2 3 4 5 6 7 8 9

Special acknowledgment to SuttaCentral for being the primary source of the suttas referenced in this book. Translations are predominantly by Bhante Sujato. Accessed throughout 2023. https://suttacentral.net/

Library of Congress Cataloging-in-Publication Data

Names: Trần, Nhi Yến Đỗ, author.
Title: Budding lotus in the west : Buddhism from an immigrant's feminist perspective / Nhi Yến Đỗ Trần.
Description: Minneapolis : Broadleaf Books, 2024. | Includes bibliographical references and index.
Identifiers: LCCN 2023053459 (print) | LCCN 2023053460 (ebook) | ISBN 9781506495149 (hardcover) | ISBN 9798889833024 (ebook)
Subjects: LCSH: Women in Buddhism. | Feminism—Religious aspects—Buddhism. | Buddhism and social problems. | Buddhism—Doctrines
Classification: LCC BQ4570.W6 T73 2024 (print) | LCC BQ4570.W6 (ebook) | DDC 294.309182/1—dc23/eng/20240108
LC record available at https://lccn.loc.gov/2023053459
LC ebook record available at https://lccn.loc.gov/2023053460

Cover design: Olga Grlic

Print ISBN: 978-1-5064-9514-9

eBook ISBN: 978-1-5064-9515-6

Printed in India.

CONTENTS

Buddhism and Feminism

1

The Feminine Light in Buddhism's Shadows

"Do elephants live in water? Can I have an iPad for my birthday? Is there a woman Buddha?" Imagine a six-year-old with sparkling brown eyes, her youthful curiosity contagious, showering you with questions that can light up a lazy Sunday. Say *xin chào* to my niece, Aurora.

One afternoon, we were curled up in my personal haven in Olympia, reading a children's book called *Grace for President.* This book is about a young Black girl named Grace who's surprised to learn that no woman has ever occupied the Oval Office in the White House. This discovery lit a fire in her to challenge societal norms. So she decides to run for president in her school's mock election.

With the painting of the Buddha's serene presence filling the room, Aurora and I traced Grace's journey through her presidential race, page by page. The climax of the story, where Grace emerges victorious by a single vote against a boy who declared himself the "best man for the job," ignited a spark in Aurora. If a girl can win a school election, why not a US presidential one? Are some roles only for men?

Her eyes, reflecting a mixture of curiosity and wonder, drifted from the Buddha painting that loomed behind me to rest on my face.

"Auntie Nhi, is there a woman Buddha?" she asked, a budding lotus in her earnest gaze.

A warm flush spread across my cheeks as I grappled with the gravity of her inquiry. In that moment, I knew that my response had the power to uplift or confine her young, hopeful spirit. I wanted to answer her honestly yet reassuringly, to both nourish and foster her blooming self-confidence.

But here's the thing. A passage in the foundational text of Theravāda Buddhism, the Pāli Canon, declares that only a man can become a buddha.[1] Meanwhile, the *Lotus Sūtra*, a revered text in Mahāyāna Buddhism, presents an alternative view. It shares the story of Śāriputra, a chief disciple of the Buddha, who doubts a dragon princess's ability to attain buddhahood, saying, "This is difficult to believe. Why? The body of a woman is filthy and not a vessel for the Dharma."

But the dragon princess isn't discouraged. Offering a precious pearl to the Buddha, she announces, "Watch as I become a Buddha!"

Then, in a swift whirlwind of transformation, she turns into a man, ventures to "the world without filth," and shortly thereafter achieves buddhahood.

Many Mahāyāna Buddhists interpret this story as evidence that women can indeed become buddhas. But there's an implicit suggestion in the story, isn't there? *Sure, women can become buddhas, but only if they first assume a male form.* This narrative perpetuates the notion that being female is a lesser state, an inadequate condition for enlightenment.

Such biases, particularly the belief that a woman's body is inherently filthy,[2] never fail to irk me. It's a misconception found in many cultures that not only strips women of their dignity but also reinforces patriarchal structures that continue to hinder gender equality. This discrimination manifests in a number of ways, including barring menstruating women from spiritual practices and community participation and perpetuating harmful taboos.

Every month, like clockwork, a woman's body prepares itself for the miracle of life. The uterine lining sheds. That's all there is to it. With the aid of modern sanitary products and proper hygiene practices, this natural process can be managed easily and efficiently, rendering any notion of "filthiness" baseless.

Far from being something impure, menstruation signifies women's remarkable ability to bring life into the world. It's a phenomenon central to human existence and evolution. Women's sacrifices in carrying and nurturing new life should be celebrated and appreciated, not diminished by ignorant and damaging stereotypes.

But I couldn't dive into all of this with Aurora just yet. Nor could I confess that the female deity of my childhood wasn't, in fact, female at all.

So I steered toward empowering narratives. "Yes, Aurora! There are many women buddhas. The most famous is the Bodhisattva of Compassion, or Bồ Tát Quan Âm in Vietnamese."

Aurora's eyes widened as she asked to see pictures. Her four-year-old sister, Aria, who had been engrossed in an iPad game, chimed in. "I want to see pictures too!"

After showing them dozens of images of Quan Âm and answering their many questions about her various forms, I led them downstairs to my parents' dining room. There, I pointed to a wooden shrine housing four statues of Quan Âm, photos of my late grandparents, several orchid plants, and fruit offerings around a lotus-engraved incense bowl.

"See," I motioned toward the top shelf, "those are all Quan Âm."

"All of them?" Aurora said, awestruck.

"Yes."

Aria, eager for a closer look, asked to be lifted. As she observed the statues, her eyes shimmered like starlight. Pointing at a Quan Âm image on an incense box, she said, "Is that her too?"

"Yes. She's so loved that she's everywhere."

At that moment, Aria's smile unfolded like a rainbow after a rain, brightening the room.

Feeling a twinge of guilt for my little fib, I watched my nieces in quiet admiration. I knew this moment would become a precious memory for them. Out of all the divine figures in the world, my parents chose to honor Quan Âm, a female bodhisattva and future buddha, a deity reflecting their own image.

But as they would inevitably grow older, they would encounter the same societal challenges and gender inequalities I faced in my youth. They'd grapple with the double standards applied to men and women and uncover the not-so-pleasant truth about Quan Âm's gender evolution. I knew their young hearts would be filled with disappointment, their world slightly darkened by the revelation. But, by that time, I hope that the girls will have the confidence they need to navigate these hidden pitfalls. Right now, as young girls with bright futures, they need to understand that their potential—and the potential of every girl and woman—was limitless. This eternal truth surpasses the constraints of any patriarchal faith.

Quan Âm was more than a mere divine figure in my life. Growing up in Việt Nam, I had always associated her with compassion, protection, and progress—a symbol of solace for men and affirmation for women, a soothing presence for those in fear or pain.

When Typhoon Noru devastated Việt Nam in 2022, several of my friends reached out to her on social media, asking for her protective grace. Two of my sisters keep amulets of Quan Âm in their cars for the same reason. One of them also has two statues of Quan Âm in her home's shrine, with the Buddha nowhere in sight.

This reverence for Quan Âm isn't exclusive to my family. Almost every Vietnamese Buddhist I've met holds her in high esteem. In fact, it wouldn't be an exaggeration to say that given the choice to honor a single deity at home, many would choose Quan Âm over the Buddha himself.

While the Buddha is revered for his wisdom, Việt Nam's history provides a unique perspective. It's a nation shaped by a tumultuous past, tasting the bitterness of enslavement, colonization, and external domination for over a thousand years. Its short fifty years of independence are but a blink of an eye compared to the long and gloomy ages preceding it. Our collective experience has been one of hardship and struggle, which is why Quan Âm's promises of compassion and relief resonate more deeply than the Buddha's path of self-enlightenment. It's not that one is superior to the other. It's just that our historical scars draw us closer to the deity who offers a balm for our wounds.

But in my twenties, I came across a startling revelation: Quan Âm wasn't always a woman. She's a Vietnamese adaptation of

Guānyīn, a female bodhisattva from China, who herself evolved from Avalokiteśvara, a bodhisattva of compassion initially depicted as a man in early Buddhist art of India.

Around the twelfth century, the Chinese transformed Avalokiteśvara into Guānyīn. And when Mahāyāna Buddhism made its way to Việt Nam, Korea, and Japan, Avalokiteśvara was mainly depicted as a woman, as the Goddess of Mercy.

In other words, Guānyīn and Quan Âm are versions of the same figure—born from Buddhist creativity and Chinese scriptures from the Six Dynasties period.

They are, in essence, not real.

My initial reaction to this discovery was a mix of emotions—disbelief, annoyance, a touch of anger. I wanted to brush it aside as a mere speculation. But, deep within me, I knew that society frequently asks women to bloom while planting them in the shade. In the Mahāyāna Buddhism that my family practices, all buddhas and bodhisattvas were men, except for Quan Âm. And now even she wasn't originally ours. Why couldn't we women have something that's truly ours, for once?

The real sting, however, wasn't just the discovery of an imaginary deity. It was the persistent sense of being considered less than men in matters of spirituality. Losing a sacred symbol felt like a paper cut compared to the soul-crushing reality of misogynistic teachings presented as the Buddha's words.

It's painful for women like me who yearn to follow in the Buddha's footsteps, only to be told that we are barred from enlightenment, are burdened by bad karma, and are the cause of the decline of Buddhism. How could we persist in a path we cherish when our efforts were considered fruitless, and our very presence accelerated its downfall? This harsh reality is the shared plight of women Buddhists worldwide.

Yet, like a bird breaking free from a cage, truth always finds a way to unfurl its wings.

The Buddha is said to have declared, "Three things cannot be long hidden: the sun, the moon, and the truth." This quote originates from a passage in the Pāli Canon that states three things shine openly for all to see, not hidden: the moon, the sun, and the Buddha's teachings.[3]

For Buddhists, the Buddha's teachings and the truth are two peas in a pod. They are one and the same. But after the Buddha's passing, the task of interpreting these teachings fell solely to the monks. As is often the case when knowledge passes through various lenses, the narrative began to shift. Women were gradually cast as lesser beings. They were painted with broad strokes, seen as prone to desire, seductive, and distracting. Their emotional complexity was viewed as instability, and their natural biological processes were misconstrued as impurity. This fostered a misguided perception that women were inherently incapable of achieving enlightenment.

These distorted views reinforced male dominance in religious circles and led to the marginalization of women within Buddhism. The most devastating impact was the pervasive sense of inferiority that seeped into the minds of women worldwide, igniting a cycle of internalized oppression that continues to echo across generations.

But as the Buddha reminds us, his teachings shine openly, like the sun's radiant glow, illuminating all without exclusion. In our modern age, we don't have to depend on monks anymore for access to the dharma. With a simple click, the scriptures are at our fingertips. Buried within these texts lies a beacon of hope—an empowering counternarrative to any discrimination imposed on women by the Buddha himself.

For the past twenty-five hundred years, what has obscured this light were human limitations and biases that twisted his teachings. The Buddha, in his radiant enlightenment and benevolence, not only welcomed everyone onto the path but also proclaimed that each of us—irrespective of gender, class, or background—holds the innate potential for enlightenment.

The truth is out there, waiting to be discovered. But it's up to us to sift through the noise, question the status quo, and turn the page to unveil what lies beneath the ink of tradition.

2

The Buddha on Spiritual Equality and Women's Enlightenment

It was a peaceful afternoon at the monastery. The sun's golden kiss was yet to retreat, and the air was drenched in the soothing scent of incense. It was one of those moments when the world outside could very well disappear, and I wouldn't have noticed. I was there, among the sea of listeners, giving the Vietnamese monk I held in high esteem my undivided attention.

He began his dharma talk by reflecting on an oddity from ancient Indian culture. "Long arms," he said, "were deeply admired. They were seen as a sign of benevolence, generosity, and extending help, an indication of a yoga practitioner's flexibility and endurance."

A curious topic, I thought, but one that stirred intrigue rather than confusion.

But then, like a sudden gust of wind toppling a house of cards, his talk veered in a direction that left me disquieted.

He associated long arms with male spiritual leaders—enlightened beings, revered yogis, and figures like the Buddha himself. Then he transitioned to naming various physical characteristics that Buddhist scriptures reserve for a "great man." And his next words, spoken with a hint of regret in his voice and a faint smile on his face, felt like an icy plunge into a winter lake. "A woman," he said, "by virtue of her form, cannot become a Buddha."

My heartbeat drummed in my ears. I glanced around the hall. Two women nearby were nodding, their smiles strained, their eyes echoing a resigned acceptance as if to say, "Maybe in our next lives, we'll be reborn as men!" The sentiment didn't seem to surprise them. Or perhaps they held the monk in such high regard that questioning his words was unthinkable.

For several seconds, my gaze lingered on these two women, as though willing them to read my mind, which was saying, "Don't believe it. It's not true!"

Despite this, my respect for the monk didn't wane. He had always been a beacon of kindness and fairness, a champion for women. I knew he was not the source of these ideas but simply the messenger. Still, that day, his light lost some of its brilliance in my eyes. For years, I had put him on a pedestal. Now he was still an inspiring figure but with a few more shades of gray.

The idea that women cannot attain buddhahood isn't new. Rather, it's an uncomfortable doctrine that many Buddhists prefer to ignore. It certainly isn't a topic that found much airtime in Western Buddhist circles as it might clash too severely with Western values of gender equality. Sure, feminist luminaries such as Jetsunma Tenzin Palmo, Bhikkhu Anālayo, and Sharon Salzberg do exist—shining like rare gemstones in a sea of tradition—but even they find it tough to rewrite the script.

Because these age-old beliefs are inked in what are considered to be the Buddha's teachings, few dare to question them, afraid of challenging the foundations of their faith.

Take, for instance, the doctrines of the Pure Land School of Buddhism, founded by a Chinese monk in the fourth century. These texts suggest that women have to give up their womanhood, transform into men, and only then can they enter the Pure Land.

The *Lotus Sūtra* further amplifies this narrative, stating that a woman who embraces its teachings will be reborn as a man in the Pure Land, free from the torments of "greed, desire, anger, rage, stupidity, or ignorance as well as the defilements of arrogance and envy."

If you're curious about the origins of this disquieting belief, I go into further detail in chapter 12.

While the demeaning portrayal of women in Buddhist literature may not be shocking to some, the implication that women are conditionally excluded from the Pure Land remains a hushed secret within the Buddhist discourse. The concept of a Land of Bliss without women, an all-male celestial paradise, often evokes a mix of reactions: alarm among male devotees, disbelief from female devotees, and general confusion for everyone else.

Imagine being a straight man who appreciates the company of women. Stumbling on this doctrinal detail might have you jump off the Pure Land train faster than Tom Cruise jumping off a motorcycle in a scene from *Mission: Impossible*.

As a feminist who embraces every aspect of my womanhood, this is more than bewildering: it's deeply disturbing. Mahāyāna Buddhism—the most widespread school of Buddhism both globally and in the United States—is the tradition followed by more than half of all Buddhists worldwide. Pure Land Buddhism is the most prominent offshoot of Mahāyāna, practiced by my ancestors, extended family, parents, siblings, and myself in my younger years. Little did we know that the final destination of this school is a place where the likes of me do not exist. Women gain entry only after assuming a male form.

The whole idea feels like a twisted joke, where the punch line falls flat, not because it lacks humor but because it's too grim to laugh at. The most tragic part is that it isn't just a poorly conceived fiction but a proposed reality accepted, embraced, and promoted by Buddhists for over a thousand years.

Breaking the Sacred Barrier

The prevailing notion that women must become men to set foot in the Pure Land is rooted in the discriminatory belief that women are fundamentally incapable of reaching the pinnacle of spiritual awakening. However—and this is a significant *however*—when we examine the early Buddhist texts (EBTs), an alternative narrative comes to light.

Imagine stars breaking through the darkness of a moonless night, countless verses that celebrate women's spiritual awakening, outshining the few that seem to undermine them.

In one such discourse, the Buddha declares that enlightenment is accessible to "any woman or man."[1] How? By navigating life's distractions and difficulties with a steady mind, cultivating skillful thoughts, being morally aware, and maintaining mindfulness. This is the Buddha's explicit endorsement of gender equality on the spiritual journey.

And he doesn't stop there. In another discourse, he outlines additional qualities that, when nurtured, can lead to enlightenment in this life. And to whom is this invitation extended? Everyone. "Monks and nuns alike," he says.[2]

The Buddha also acknowledges the significant number of nuns who have achieved the "undefiled freedom of heart" and "freedom by wisdom."[3] These terms mean that they have reached liberation through serenity and insight, residing in a state of ultimate peace and bliss. In other words, they have achieved enlightenment.

Consider, also, the conversation between the Buddha and Visākhā, a wealthy and influential woman regarded as his chief female patron. The Buddha explains to her that a woman is accomplished in wisdom when she possesses "the understanding of arising and passing away which is noble, penetrative, and leads to the complete ending of suffering."[4] To the Buddha, the "complete ending of suffering" is the same as attaining enlightenment, or *nirvāṇa,* signifying the extinguishing of greed, hate, and delusion, which cause suffering.

The Buddha says he doesn't make enlightenment declarations to comfort his disciples. His intent is to inspire others, to show them that they, too, could discover lasting happiness and inner peace. He says, "Imagine a nun who's learned that another nun has reached enlightenment. She knows firsthand, or she's heard from someone else, that that sister had such ethics, such qualities, such wisdom, such meditation, or such freedom. Remembering this, she applies her mind to that end. And that is how a nun lives at ease."[5]

This approach is how our parents, teachers, or coaches drummed stories of trailblazers into our heads, hoping to inspire us. This particular teaching isn't just another illustration of the Buddha's recognition and cheerleading for women's ability to reach enlightenment but a rallying call for all of us to lace up our boots and give it a go.

Let's take a step back to a moment when the Buddha praises a devoted housewife who comforts her sick husband with the teachings of the dharma. The Buddha says to the husband, "You're fortunate, householder. So very fortunate to have such a wise woman at your side to advise and instruct you out of kindness and compassion."[6]

This isn't merely a heartwarming story. It's a spotlight on the Buddha's respect and appreciation for spiritual insight, transcending societal ranks or gender constructs. The Buddha recognizes wisdom everywhere and in everyone—not just monks or nuns but also lay practitioners like this caring woman. For him, wisdom isn't a private club for a select few. It's up for grabs for anyone ready to dive in. When we display such wisdom, the Buddha commends us—women or not.

Let's think about this teaching too: wisdom is the fruit of thoughtful reflection, learning, and meditation.[7] It springs from virtues such as ethical behavior, contentment, restraint, mindfulness, and awareness.[8] Are these traits checking your ID for gender before they decide to show up? No. Each and every one of us carries within us the seeds of these virtues, ready to bloom under the right conditions.

The Legacy of Elder Nuns

If you're new to the depths of Buddhist literature, you might not know about the Therīgāthā, or "Verses of the Elder Nuns." But you should. This collection—part of the Pāli Canon—gives voice to seventy-three women from the Buddha's time. They're vivid accounts of struggle, triumph, and spiritual insight.

Imagine opening a book and encountering inspiring women like Khemā, Dhammā, and Sundarī, all sharing their liberation experience from various forms of suffering.[9] As we turn the pages, we meet Cīrā, Sukkā, and Bhaddā, each detailing her own breakthrough from life's tangles.[10]

Then we step into the lives of more nuns who immersed themselves in the depths of knowledge, gaining profound insight into the truths of existence.[11]

Through yet another lens, we glimpse stories of women finding peace and solace amid life's storms, discovering lasting joy, snipping the cords of sorrow, overcoming cravings, and embracing the power of letting go.[12]

Parallel to this, several other nuns charted the path of spiritual liberation, achieving deep-rooted peace and unparalleled tranquility.[13]

Last, we witness the resilience of various nuns who free themselves from the defilements that held back their spiritual evolution.[14]

Together, these narratives shape an expansive, spirited understanding of women's spiritual awakening. And there's more. We also find thirty nuns reaching enlightenment under the guidance of Paṭācārā.[15] This enlightened nun leads an assembly of over five hundred followers, further amplifying the strides these women make on their collective journey toward enlightenment.

These stories, combined with the Buddha's recognition of his foremost nuns in thirteen distinct categories, make a compelling case. They not only highlight the influential spiritual legacy left by these women but also echo across time and space.

Take, for example, a revealing moment when Visākha, a layman, approached the Buddha for validation after hearing an extensive teaching from a nun named Dhammadinnā, the foremost of his female disciples in the category of "expounding the Dharma." Visākha was like a student checking his homework against the teacher's answer key. And what was the Buddha's response? He praised Dhammadinnā as a wellspring of great wisdom, stating that he would have answered "exactly the same way she did."[16]

This statement underscores the Buddha's conviction that not only could women reach the pinnacle of spiritual awakening, but they could also teach the dharma with as much depth and clarity as he could. It echoes loudly through the corridors of time, challenging us to shatter any lingering glass ceilings in our own understanding: Wisdom knows no gender; enlightenment is not a privilege—it's everyone's birthright.

The Contradiction in Texts and Its Societal Roots

While the Buddha's teachings affirm the equality of spiritual potential across genders, they appear to conflict with other passages. To delve deeper into this paradox, let's examine the Pāli text that stands in sharp contrast in its entirety: "It's impossible for a woman to be a perfected one, a fully awakened Buddha. But it's possible for a man to be a perfected one, a fully awakened Buddha. It's impossible for a woman to be a wheel-turning monarch. But it's possible for a man to be a wheel-turning monarch. It's impossible for a woman to perform the role of Sakka, Māra, or Brahmā. But it's possible for a man to perform the role of Sakka, Māra, or Brahmā."[17]

Modern scholars generally interpret Sakka (the king of the gods), Māra (the king of demons, or the "Tempter"), and Brahmā (the "great god") more as literary constructs than job titles found on LinkedIn. Given that these texts were written by and primarily for men in a patriarchal society, it's hardly surprising that they reserve roles of power exclusively for men.

In some Buddhist traditions, there are contentions that women can attain arahantship—or perfection, the last state of enlightenment—but not reach the status of a "fully awakened Buddha" or a samyaksambuddha, a being who attains enlightenment without a teacher, discovers the forgotten dharma, and then shares it with others. The historical Buddha is an example of a samyaksambuddha.

But within the EBTs, any elevated status attributed to him likely stems from social constructs spun by followers to add more intrigue and prestige to his image. At its core, the term *Buddha* simply means "the awakened one." He "awakens" to the reality of existence, to the truth of suffering and the path leading away from it, much like pulling back a curtain to let the light flood in. This awakening—this realization, this enlightenment—is not confined to one person, one gender, or one social status. It's a potential within each of us, waiting to be stirred. It's a transformative insight that, like the Buddha, we are all capable of uncovering.

The Buddha says, "'Ascetic,' 'Brahmin,' 'Knowledge Master,' 'Healer,' 'Unstained,' 'Immaculate,' 'Knower,' and 'Freed' are terms for the Realized One, the Arahant, the fully awakened Buddha."[18] This teaching highlights that the Buddha sees no distinction between an arahant—one who has achieved arahantship—and a fully awakened buddha.

Furthermore, in several discourses, the label *freed* is often used to describe enlightened nuns. By the Buddha's own terminology above, enlightened nuns can thus be considered fully awakened buddhas. He once said that a group of nuns is "well freed without anything left over."[19] In essence, they reach complete enlightenment, where all forms of greed, ignorance, and desire have been fully eradicated from the mind.

The Buddha's Universal Path to Enlightenment

The Buddha's teachings consistently underscored the fundamental unity of humanity, rejecting discrimination based on social status, birth, or physical attributes. He regards any divisions or disparities among humans as being as fleeting as morning dew—ready to dissipate under the warm gaze of the dawning sun. In his own words:

> The differences between humans are not defined by birth.
> Not by hair nor by head, not by ear nor by eye,
> not by mouth nor by nose, not by lips nor by eyebrow,
> not by shoulder nor by neck, not by belly nor by back,
> not by buttocks nor by breast, not by groin nor by genitals,
> not by hands nor by feet, not by fingers nor by nails,
> not by knees nor by thighs, not by color nor by voice:
> none of these are defined by birth as it is for other species.
> In individual human bodies, you can't find such distinctions.
> The distinctions among humans are spoken of by convention.[20]

In articulating this, the Buddha makes it clear that our true worth and potential come from within, uninfluenced by shallow differences. He elaborates on the real essence of our spiritual journey:

> Deeds keep the world turning, deeds keep people moving;
> we're all tied up by our actions, like a moving chariot's linchpin.
> By austerity and spiritual practice, by restraint and by self-control:
> that's how to become a Brahmin, this is the supreme Brahmin.

In essence, our journey toward enlightenment is crafted by our deliberate, ethical actions, not by labels or birthrights. Embracing this teaching means we must reject any preconceived notions about who is or isn't capable of reaching full enlightenment. To claim Buddhism as a pathway to inner transformation while simultaneously making judgments based on gender or physical attributes is to fundamentally misunderstand the Buddha's teachings.

Let's circle back once more to that confounding passage earlier—the one asserting that it's impossible for women to become fully awakened buddhas. This passage is part of a long discourse that kicks off with the Buddha emphasizing that astuteness is the key to avoiding danger, while foolishness is like inviting trouble by walking around with a "kick me" sign on our backs.

Naturally, Ānanda, the Buddha's attendant, wants to know how one becomes astute. The Buddha notes there are countless ways, including understanding consciousness, grasping ignorance, and learning about the six sense fields and dependent origination.

The Buddha then touches on how to discern the possible from the impossible. He advises that a spiritual seeker should understand that nothing is permanent. That we can't perceive anything as self. That good and bad conduct reap consequences. That certain actions—like causing harm or creating division—are impossible for an enlightened person to do.

Then, out of nowhere, the discourse takes a sharp turn. The verse in question suddenly appears, asserting that it's impossible for a woman to become a fully awakened buddha. This claim stands out like a jagged rock disrupting the flow of a calm river. It's jarring. It doesn't harmonize with the other teachings within the same sutta, particularly the Buddha's foundational doctrine of not-self.

In one breath, he urges us not to identify with any form or identity—whether internal, like biological traits, or external, like social roles and labels, from the past or present, rough or smooth, or better or worse than something else. The essence of not-self is to guide us toward transcending ego, possessiveness, and conceit.[21]

Yet in the next breath, he appears to suggest that a woman—whose identity is shaped by both biological traits and social constructs—faces limitations in spiritual roles, unlike a man.

This disconcerting passage—and other texts seemingly brimming with misogyny—suggest that the redactors and authors themselves might have been tangled up in their own self-view. Instead of embodying the practice of not-self, they appeared intent on inflating men's ego, possessiveness, and conceit—the very traits the Buddha disapproved of.

Such recognition showed that even the most distinguished monks weren't immune to human flaws and the sway of patriarchal norms. It highlighted the need for deep introspection—to scrutinize our beliefs, actions, and social environment. To identify and challenge any biases we might be unknowingly carrying around like extra baggage in our own pursuit of spiritual growth.

As we move forward, let's hold on to the wise words of the nun Somā, a trailblazer in her own right. When Māra tries to deter her from the path, asserting that women's wisdom was weak and inadequate, she fires back, "What difference does womanhood make when the mind is serene, and knowledge is present as you rightly discern the Dharma. Surely, someone who might think, 'I am woman,' or 'I am man,' or 'I am' anything at all, is fit for Māra to address."[22]

Somā's words, centuries old yet still as relevant as ever, inspire us to question, challenge, and shatter the barriers created by societal expectations and prejudices.

The Buddha himself emphasizes the freedom of nonidentification: "When you identify with form, you're bound by Māra. Not identifying, you're free."[23]

Sit with that for a moment. It's an open challenge to liberate ourselves from the identities and labels that hold us back.

We are not our bodies, thoughts, emotions, or experiences. We are the *more* in *so much more.*

Each and every single one of us—we are free.

3

The Murky Waters of Love in the Sangha

Since early adulthood, monastic life has called to me like a half-remembered song—faint yet familiar. Four times, I worked up the courage to seek ordination. And four times, I drifted off course, caught in complicated currents of romantic attraction.

First attempt, August 2010.

Boarding a plane to Việt Nam, my heart swelled with anticipation. For years, I'd been engrossed in the teachings of Venerable Thích Nhật Từ, a prolific author of over seventy books and an intellectual powerhouse committed to spreading Buddhist teachings through education and charity. I'd soaked up his wisdom online through his dharma talks and written works. Now, the prospect of meeting him in person filled me with a sense of awe and excitement.

After attending one of his dharma talks, I summoned the courage to discuss becoming his disciple. He seemed encouraging and directed me to the Việt Nam Buddhist Institute, where he served as vice rector, to pick up an application.

So there I was, the next day, filled with anxious optimism, walking up to the administrative desk where an elderly Vietnamese woman, her hair a neat cascade of black and clad in a white short-sleeved dress shirt, regarded me with an experienced, discerning look.

"You're not a nun, so you need a master's degree to apply," she said flatly as if telling me they were out of sugar.

"But the Venerable said a bachelor's degree would do," I countered.

"No. You misheard him. You need a master's degree."

The weight of her words settled in, leaving me in a momentary state of disbelief and disappointment. Stepping out into the bustling streets of Sài Gòn, I felt adrift in a sea of confusion. Motorbikes zipped by in a chaotic ballet, indifferent to my inner turmoil. What was I to do now? Return to Seattle for a master's degree?

Then, like a sudden break in the clouds, it struck me—Báo Quốc Buddhist Academy. The monastic training center in Huế, my parents' hometown, where Zen Master Thích Nhất Hạnh and my great-uncle the Venerable Thích Viên Giác had received their training. A place that might, just might, have different rules. Fueled by this glimmer of hope, I booked a flight there for the next day.

Two weeks later, thanks to an introduction from a close friend, I found myself soaking up the local spiritual culture. My guide offered to zip me around on his bike to any landmarks I wished to visit. He was tall, a bit shy, undeniably handsome, and spoke with the Huế accent that felt like home to me. One fateful day, as we stood beside the Perfume River, where the water flowed in harmony with the universe, he turned to me and said,

"Would you consider giving me a chance before giving up the lay life?"

I was twenty-three and had felt the intoxicating pull of romance before but never the profound depth of love. His words struck a new chord in my heart, one that resonated differently than anything I'd felt before. With a smile that likely betrayed more than casual interest, I said, "Okay."

Our relationship lasted three years.

Fast-forward to the third attempt—I'll circle back to the second in a moment; it's quite the yarn. It was December 2021. I was in Edmonton, Canada, braving the winter chill at a week-long meditation retreat led by the Venerable Thích Pháp Hòa. He was something of a spiritual rock star within the Vietnamese diaspora. Holding him in high esteem, much like my family and most Vietnamese Buddhists I knew, I decided to share my aspiration to become his disciple during a one-on-one consultation on the fifth day of the retreat.

His response was a gut punch: "I don't accept female disciples anymore."

I asked him why. His explanation boiled down to space constraints at the monastery, his frequent travel, and his belief that he could engage more candidly and freely with monks than nuns. "There are many delicate matters that I find myself unable to share with the nuns, but I can with monks," he said. Then he suggested that I embark on my monastic journey at a nunnery, reasoning that a supportive community of senior nuns would serve as a more beneficial environment.

I supposed the silver lining after the rejection was that he seemed to take a special interest in me. I found myself the recipient of more attention, more jokes, more kindness—it was like getting a consolation prize, if you will. So, despite my disappointment, I was grateful for his efforts to soften the blow.

By the time I returned to Seattle, my mind had wandered to a different space—or, rather, to a different person. A monk at the retreat—a disciple of the Venerable—had offered a song during the last evening, his mesmerizing voice weaving a melody that stuck in my head. I found myself repeatedly replaying the scene, remembering his gentle face and warm, hesitant smile. His aura, his *je ne sais quoi*, stirred my heart. I realized then that if I had become his spiritual sibling, his presence would have been a constant distraction. So perhaps it was a blessing in disguise that things didn't work out.

Gliding to the fourth attempt: October 2022. There I was, at Delhi airport, awaiting the arrival of the Venerable Thích Nhật Từ and an entourage of 150 individuals, set to embark on a Buddhist pilgrimage through India and Nepal. Now at thirty-five, I wondered if the Venerable would remember me from our previous encounter.

Following our meeting in 2010, I had turned to Facebook to share his teachings. I figured the least I could do was spread his wisdom virtually. To my surprise, months later, the Venerable instructed his attendant, Thầy Ngộ Dũng, to get in touch with me to help manage the Facebook page. What started as a modest community of four hundred followers has now grown to over a million—a milestone that underscores the Venerable's broad appeal and the universal resonance of his teachings.

This pilgrimage, a dozen years after our first meeting, felt like a chance for discipleship redemption, possibly my last shot at becoming a nun. The Buddha attained enlightenment at thirty-five; and here I was, the same age, but still figuring out how to get it all started. My plan was to feel things out for a few days, and if the Venerable seemed receptive toward me, I'd muster the courage to bring up my aspiration once more.

While I was lost in these thoughts, an Indian man wearing worn-in dark blue jeans and a rich maroon shirt ambled over, breaking my reverie with his infectious energy. He mentioned he was waiting for his navy pals and, with an easy confidence, suggested we go grab a cup of coffee. His eyes, dark and endless as a night sky, held a magnetic pull. My stomach fluttered like a butterfly caught in the breeze, and before I knew it, I found myself nodding in agreement.

Half an hour later, we had exchanged numbers, and I was scrambling to meet the arriving pilgrims. Despite a packed schedule in the following two weeks, I managed to sneak in two more rendezvous with the Maroon Mariner. The path this was taking was as clear as a foggy Seattle morning, yet I found myself content to ride the wave, adopting the attitude of "whatever happens, happens."

The ripples of my encounters with the Maroon Mariner had barely settled when a new tide seemed to roll in on the third day of the pilgrimage. A young Vietnamese-Swede man, who originally sat a few seats away on our assigned bus number four, gradually navigated his way into the seat right next to me. It felt like watching a shadow get longer as the day went on—unnoticeable at first until he became a constant presence throughout the rest of the pilgrimage.

Several days later, after a communal breakfast bathed in the early light, I took a chance and asked Thầy Ngộ Dũng if I could switch to bus one, the vehicle of choice for the Venerable. He consented. Relieved, I found a spot next to a senior lady with hair like a monochrome ocean—curly, salt and pepper. She was full of stories about Vietnamese herbal medicines, but apart from this specific enthusiasm, she was mostly silent.

The refuge I'd found was short-lived. That afternoon, my bus-four buddy popped up, catching me off guard with a question that was as straightforward as you could get: "Are you avoiding me?"

"No," I said, trying to shield him from any sting. "I just wanted to spend more time with the Venerable to learn from him," I explained, a half-truth. The Venerable was like an encyclopedia of pilgrimage stories and the Buddha's teachings. A day prior, when he accompanied us on bus four, he'd shared his wealth of knowledge generously, making our hours-long ride significantly more insightful and rewarding.

"Are you sure?" His gaze swirling with skepticism.

"Yeah," I responded with gentle assurance. A moment lingered as I thought of how to convey a deeper truth. "You know, in Buddhism, we're encouraged to practice nondiscrimination. So I try to have no preferences about who I sit next to. I'm just here to learn from the Venerable."

His eyes, a calm pool reflecting a ripple of disappointment, met mine before he nodded slowly.

"Okay," he said. "I'll let you be, then."

As he walked away, I let out a sigh—part relief, part guilt. Disappointing someone always left an uncomfortable knot in my chest, but the stakes were high. I didn't want to give the wrong impression to the Venerable.

The next day, however, the familiar face from bus four reappeared, stating that he, too, wanted to learn from the Venerable. I couldn't help but wonder if my hint yesterday just whooshed right over his head. Still, I responded with a warm smile and scooted over, making room for him. Then, as if on cue, in walked the lady with the cool hair, and suddenly, we were all playing this awkward game of musical chairs, trying to figure out what to do with two extra people when there was only room for one. Eventually, with apologetic looks toward the bus-one passengers, we retreated back to bus four.

As I passed by the Venerable, our glances briefly caught each other's—a snapshot of time where a wave of mild anxiety and embarrassment swept over me. In the seconds our eyes connected, I couldn't help but wonder what the Venerable made of this little spectacle.

As it turns out, the Venerable did remember me. One morning during breakfast, he gave me an unexpected shoutout, acknowledging my contribution to the creation of his Facebook page. Over the following days, he invited me to join him for photos at the Buddha's birthplace and other significant sites. I began to feel hopeful, almost confident, that he would support my aspiration. All I needed to do was keep on the straight and narrow, maintain a respectful distance from my Việt-Swede companion, and ensure my conduct was impeccable.

But then, one evening during dinner, Thầy Ngộ Dũng revealed that while the Venerable did accept female disciples, they were usually relocated to his other temples as his residence was exclusively for male monks. The news took my breath away. The thought of becoming a disciple without the physical presence of my teacher seemed as fruitful as a tree without sunlight.

And with that revelation, my fourth—and final?—attempt fizzled out.

Now, let's flash back to my second bid, a chapter where I invested my heart and soul.

Spring 2017 unfurled its petals as I wheeled my luggage across a scenic vista of gold and green, having landed in the serenity of a monastery founded by Zen Master Thích Nhất Hạnh. Cradled within the embrace of El Paso, this spiritual haven had cast a spell on me during a weeklong retreat the previous year. Now I was returning with the sun smiling warmly on me for a yearlong residential internship. I was heartened by the idea of practicing alongside the nuns, potentially becoming one of them. Imagine the thrill of your first day at your dream job—excitement fizzing like champagne bubbles, anticipation sweet as the first drop of nectar. That was me, whispering to the wind as I stepped onto the hallowed grounds, "I am finally here. I am home!"

The first five weeks were a blur, a delightful whirlwind where I savored every moment of every day. I was surrounded by the kindest souls, with abundant opportunities for practice and learning. From staffing retreats and participating in Q&A panels to forging close bonds with my fellow interns and many of the nuns, my days were full of joy, discovery, and meaning.

Week six, however, brought with it an unexpected curveball. A monk with nine vassas—or nine years of monastic life—under his belt gifted me a red book titled *Happiness Is . . . 500 Ways to Show I Love You.*

Not long after, another monk, a novice with only two vassas, used a medley of gestures and a Vietnamese classic—"Và Con Tim Đã Vui Trở Lại" ("And the Heart Is Happy Again")—to express his feelings.

It was as though I had stumbled into a Korean drama, minus the luxury of a script or director's guidance. Back in Seattle, evading unwanted attention was as simple as ignoring calls or texts. Here, in the monastery's communal setting, avoiding the emerging romantic tension was like walking a tightrope. The red-book monk made it a point to openly show his affection for me in front of his monastic brothers, as if marking his territory or warning off competition. His message was so clear that several times, while engaging in conversations with me, the brothers would promptly excuse themselves as soon as he appeared, not wanting to incur his displeasure.

In an earnest effort to maintain a practice of nondiscrimination and to quell any potential gossip, I tried to interact with all the brothers and laymen on equal footing, giving no special attention to any individual. I also took the opportunity to convey to the red-book monk that my internship at the monastery marked a departure from any romantic aspirations I might have had. While he seemed to understand at first, he eventually lapsed back into his previous patterns.

By month three, I was convinced that the entire monastery was aware of the unfolding situation. And, come month four, the rug was pulled from under my feet. The senior nuns handed down nine rules that were not only designed to limit female interactions with monks and laymen but also to enforce a stricter communal discipline. While some rules were specifically for me, the majority applied to all women, including the nuns themselves.

These rules varied widely, from barring me from hiking with a nun to requiring a "second body" to accompany me during conversations with monks. Even simple activities, like taking a hike on monastery grounds, now required approval from our mentor. Once given the go-ahead, we also had to note our names, destinations, and reasons on a kitchen whiteboard.

A senior sister's words still ring clear in my memory as she explained the first two rules: "We are not worried about you. The brothers are young, and their practice is still not solid, so we want to do all we can to support them."

If you're looking for an example of how patriarchy becomes internalized, leading women to become its enforcers, there you have it. The nuns rarely held the monks accountable. The monks, free from similar rules designed to "support" us women, went about their days as they pleased.

It's worth noting that the "second body" system is a longstanding practice at Thích Nhất Hạnh's monasteries, but its application often left much to be desired. Thích Nhất Hạnh's book, *Happiness: Essential Mindfulness Practice*, describes a second body as someone who looks after another when they are physically ill, afflicted in mind, or overworked. This individual offers special care and concern, not a police officer keeping watch over one's activities. But at this monastery, the system felt more like the latter. Even short-term women residents—those staying for three days or a week—were told to bring a second body when visiting the monks' hamlet. It remained unclear whether this guidance extended to monks and laymen, but from my vantage point, many monks seemed to flout this rule with impunity, creating awkward encounters that I had to tactfully navigate.

During my tenure there, Thích Nhất Hạnh was in Việt Nam, so I couldn't seek his guidance on these issues. But as the days stretched on, the tension of reconciling these contradictory practices, the weight of the inequities, and my growing sense of voicelessness became increasingly unbearable. It led me to reconsider the path and this community that I had once cherished.

One afternoon, I found myself on a secluded hilltop, dissolving into tears in the arms of a senior nun who had been like a sister and mentor to me. My fellow interns sat beside us, their faces etched with concern. As time blurred, stretching into two, maybe three hours, each tear that escaped seemed to carry away a fragment of my spirit, leaving behind a hollow I wasn't sure could ever be filled.

These weren't just tears of sorrow or frustration; they were tears of self-reproach and regret. Unlike many nuns who had endured similar struggles and pressed on, I realized I had reached my limit. The Buddha's teachings had always urged us to cultivate an inner resilience capable of weathering life's harshest storms, yet here I was, surrendering to mine. I felt a deep sorrow for abandoning this spiritual path, and for disappointing my fellow interns and the monastics who had invested their faith in me. In a community where I yearned for liberation, happiness, and peace, I found a stifling atmosphere of mistrust and hierarchy, and it broke me.

A Stark Example of Female Agency

In the EBTs, there's a story about a young nun named Subhā and a man trying to woo her. He showers her with compliments about her youthful beauty, such as, "You're young and flawless. Your eyes are as beautiful as a deer's or a mountain pixie's. What will going forth do for you? Put away the robe, let's go play among the flowers."

But Subhā doesn't fall for his words. She tells him about the Buddha's teachings, and how they liberate her from desire. But the man doesn't get it and persists in his pursuit, so she takes a drastic step—she plucks out one of her eyes and gives it to him.[1]

This unsettling story serves as a reminder of the lengths women go to in order to fend off unwanted advances. Even now, it reflects the disproportionate measures women are culturally compelled to adopt to protect men from their own impulses.

This can range from wearing modest attire to covering hair or refraining from eating certain fruits in public.

What's unfortunate is how often women are the enforcers of these norms, policing each other to adhere to a standard of "modesty" or "appropriate behavior," essentially participating in their own oppression. All the while, the Buddha's teachings did not put the burden of control solely on women.

In Buddhism, desire is seen as a wildfire, something e-v-e-r-y-o-n-e can tame with discipline. If men can't control their impulses, it's perceived as a mental weakness. Like a weak branch giving in to a storm. Asking women to limit our freedom and adjust our behavior to accommodate men's lack of control is not just unfair; it's an act of cowardice on the part of men who demand it. If any community—Buddhist or otherwise—imposes restrictive rules on one gender while the other gets a free pass, they need to ask themselves: Are we perpetuating a sexist culture? Are we truly pushing for equality? Or are we just tightening the chains that hold everyone back?

Sexism, or any power imbalance, needs to be called out wherever it rears its head, even within a spiritual community. When we stay quiet or fail to act, perhaps because it benefits us or makes us comfortable, we must ask ourselves: What does this silence say about our morality? Our courage? And our commitment to justice and equality?

In the realm of spiritual communion, the aspirations and respect for each individual should be paramount. This was my hope and expectation when I started my residential internship. I was transparent about my intentions from the onset, seeking a community that would nurture rather than hinder my calling. Yet I found myself facing multiple layers of restrictions and limitations.

When someone from the sangha—the community of nuns, monks, and laypeople practicing together—feels the call to monasticism, we should treasure their decision as if it were a rare gem, protecting their journey from any shadow of doubt, regardless of gender. In fact, the struggles of women to gain acceptance within the sangha have historically been fraught with obstacles, making it even more crucial to honor, support, and protect their decisions.

Transcending Desire with Practical Buddhist Teachings

The Buddha offers numerous teachings on transcending desire and attachment to achieve a state of inner peace and joy, particularly when it comes to the opposite sex. Monks are encouraged to see women of different ages as their own mothers, sisters, and daughters—and the same principle applies to nuns.[2] If that approach falls short, the Buddha suggests thinking about the less appealing aspects of the body—such as feces, bile, mucus, and pus—to help let go of sensual attachment. Alternatively, we can choose to guard our senses and exercise restraint in what we see, hear, smell, taste, feel, and think about.

The Buddha teaches, "The world's pretty things aren't sensual pleasures. Greedy intention is a person's sensual pleasure. The world's pretty things stay just as they are, but a wise one removes desire for them."[3]

I deeply appreciate this teaching because it shifts the locus of control back to us. It's not the shiny iPhone or the latest Jordans that get us all tangled up; it's our fixation on them. When we're craving a tiramisu cake while trying to lose weight, it's the craving, not the cake, that gets us into trouble.

Feelings and doubts can indeed emerge without warning, catching us off guard. I've experienced that too. But when someone is drawn toward the path of monasticism, it's their gentle way of drawing a boundary. This should be respected without question. To push against this boundary for the sake of our own feelings or desires is not just selfish; it's a misunderstanding of the essence of the spiritual path.

Taking a moment to consider this is worthwhile: Can our individual affection for someone truly surpass the spiritual nourishment they find on their chosen path? The answer, more often than not, is no. While romantic love can be deeply fulfilling, it tends to be specific and sometimes transient, contrasting with the expansive, enduring love found in spiritual practice. This broader love, which extends to all sentient and insentient beings, is not only long-lasting but also offers a sense of freedom and boundlessness.

Moreover, we should be mindful not to place our feelings above those of others. Through the lens of not-self, they bear no weight at all. Don't let something as fleeting and unreliable as feelings impede someone else's spiritual journey.

The Buddha also states, "Freedom of heart comes from the fading away of greed, while freedom by wisdom comes from the fading away of ignorance."[4] There's a kind of simplicity in this understanding—there's no emotional hangover from not getting something we never craved in the first place. The mind is the battleground where our true challenges unfold. We are not passive victims of temptation; we are active participants in our own emotional and spiritual states. The keys to contentment and freedom are within our grasp, literally a thought away.

The Value of Spiritual Friendship

The Buddha places spiritual friendships in high regard, viewing them as allies on the path to spiritual growth. With good, supportive spiritual friends, we can expect a life rooted in ethics, wisdom, and energetic pursuit, as well as meaningful conversations that help "open up the heart."[5]

He says that a good spiritual friend is like a sturdy tree that stands firm in the face of a raging storm, enduring what others find hard to bear. They give when it's tough and do what's hard. They stand by us through thick and thin. They're a vault for our deepest secrets, and they trust us enough to share their own. Even when life throws curveballs, they're not the kind to abandon us or look down on us.[6]

The Buddha further illuminates the qualities of an ideal friend. Such a person is not only likable and agreeable but also a source of joy and comfort in our life. They command respect and admiration, with their actions and words reflecting a deep sense of wisdom and integrity. They're not afraid to gently correct us when we veer off course and are open to receive the same from us. They engage in deep conversations that nourish our hearts and would never push us toward harmful behavior.[7]

Imagine practicing in a sangha where everyone embodies these ideal qualities, where each person is "likable and agreeable," a source of joy and comfort in our life. If such a sangha exists, please send me the coordinates—I'll join pronto!

Bridging from this idyllic vision to the reality of our interconnected lives, it becomes clear why, in a sangha, the foundation of every meaningful bond is a genuine spiritual friendship. It is on the bedrock of this friendship that we build a sanctuary—strong enough to withstand any emotional or spiritual hurdles that come our way. If love blossoms in this environment, it's because the soil is fertile, nurtured by mutual respect, shared values, and common spiritual goals.

Finding Balance in Love and Spirituality

The teachings of the Buddha offer valuable insights into the nature of romantic bonds. He underscores the need for deep conversations, deep listening, and deep insight into another's life journey—endeavors that demand time and patience. He advises, "By living with them, we can discern a person's ethics. By dealing with them, we can perceive a person's purity. By observing their conduct during tough times, we can measure a person's resilience. Through discussion, we can uncover a person's wisdom. However, all this requires time, attentiveness, and prudence."[8]

This teaching suggests that the intoxicating whirlwind of new romance, which can swiftly carry us away, should be seen as a sign—a signal to slow down. In the early flush of love, we're like sailors navigating a tumultuous sea, blinded by infatuation, often failing to see the person for who they really are. Just as a sailor must carefully chart a course to avoid the perils hidden beneath the waves, we must anchor our hearts with intention. A rush of emotions, while exhilarating, can misguide us toward a harbor of regret, leaving our relationship in disarray like a ship dashed against the cliffs.

Furthermore, love calls for a dual awareness—an understanding of the other and a keen introspection of the self. Falling in love—an emotional state that can change as swiftly as the wind—is one thing, while offering love—a thoughtful, selfless commitment to the other person's happiness—is another. To offer such love goes beyond fleeting feelings; it requires deep understanding, steadfast dedication, and a focused heart. Anchored in trust, respect, and open communication, this form of love becomes a catalyst, inspiring us to evolve into our best selves. Without these anchors, the ship of our relationship risks sinking into the uncertain depths of jealousy, doubt, and insecurity.

Thích Nhất Hạnh once illuminated that the highest form of love respects and honors the other person's independence and freedom, creating a space for them to thrive uniquely. In contrast to possessive or controlling love, true love embodies patience, understanding, and compassion. This is the love that the Buddha envisions for us—one that doesn't just weather the storms but thrives in them, offering a beacon of shared strength and warmth.

The Buddha teaches that for a flourishing relationship, partners should be equal in faith, ethics, generosity, and wisdom.[9] Couples should balance each other well, living righteously and faithfully and being generous and disciplined. This harmony of qualities fosters an environment where love can mature and thrive.

In the Buddha's era, power was generally held by men, while women's rights were significantly restricted. But the Buddha presented a vision of balance and equality. He recognized the intrinsic value of both men and women, emphasizing the significance of each partner's contributions to the relationship. He teaches that men should honor, respect, and support their wives. Women should also take a leading role, especially in managing the household and financial resources. While this might seem like a nod toward traditional gender roles, at its heart, the Buddha was advocating for a relationship built on mutual respect, shared responsibility, and trust. He also underscored the importance of fidelity—viewing it as a central pillar of a strong partnership, the bedrock on which trust is built, and the anchor to a lasting relationship.[10]

These ideas find a striking resonance today, where swiping right has become a norm, and the idea of sticking with one person feels almost vintage. We live in a time when hook-up culture has taken center stage and being loyal in a relationship is increasingly rare. Yet fidelity remains the secret ingredient that keeps a relationship from falling apart. When that is lost, the foundation of trust crumbles and everything else tends to unravel.

Applying the Buddha's timeless wisdom to my own life, I've endeavored to create relationships rooted in this same equality, respect, and trust. It's about genuinely knowing each other and building a partnership that thrives on individuality and mutual support.

But I'll be honest with you: it's been tough. As you've come to know, I've been on the verge of committing to a monastic existence multiple times, but I've also been in relationships that I hoped would stand the test of time.

Spoiler: they didn't.

My longest romantic commitment lasted three years, and I can't help but think that the three thousand miles between us somehow kept the love fresh or at least kept us from driving each other crazy.

Most of my other romances? About a year. I often joke about it with friends, but deep down, it's a hard truth: I haven't cracked the code on making love last. So as much as I would like to end this chapter with a nugget of wisdom from personal success, I can't. I could only share some of the Buddha's wisdom and hope it serves you well.

At the time I'm writing this, I've hit thirty-six, and in Vietnamese culture, that's what they call *ế*, or "past your prime." Some may wince at the term, but I've chosen to wear it like a badge of humorous honor. I'm at peace with the idea of never marrying, never having kids, and even letting go of my monastic aspirations. My happiness isn't tied to these roles or milestones. In fact, there are moments when I feel like I've hit the jackpot—graced with freedom and leisure time that some of my peers might envy.

The purpose of writing this chapter isn't to pass judgment on or point fingers at any community. I recognize that much of our behavior is shaped by our upbringing and societal norms. Yet it's important to remember that the Buddha offered clear guidelines on the kinds of relationships that should flourish within spiritual settings, emphasizing the qualities that make the sangha a genuine refuge.

Whether we find ourselves in a spiritual community or wrestling with the intricacies of love in a secular world, the Buddha's wisdom remains a beacon. Love is a powerful force that can upend our lives and send us spiraling into a cyclone of emotions and decisions. It's easy to get lost, to make choices impulsively, and to forget the person we are or strive to be. Let us hold fast to our highest values, acting with courage, compassion, and wisdom. As we navigate the complexities of love and life, may we never lose sight of that far-off shore—a sanctuary of freedom, peace, and equanimity unbound by life's shifting sands.

4

Abortion

What Would the Buddha Say?

My Buddhist upbringing instilled in me the belief that abortion violates the first precept—refrain from taking life. I accepted it, understanding its place within the Buddhist ethical framework. However, when I found myself possibly pregnant in my midtwenties, my gut response was immediate and decisive: "Nope, no way. Not ready." Though the pregnancy test, thankfully, never confirmed my fears, the clarity of my choice remained—I would choose abortion rather than venture unprepared into the daunting realm of motherhood.

Abortion is a topic that ignites fiery debates, sending waves of passion and discord across America, although it hasn't always stirred such intense controversy.

For half a century, *Roe v. Wade* stood as firm as a mighty oak, protecting the legality of abortion in the nation. But in June 2022, that formidable tree toppled. The US Supreme Court overturned the ruling, tossing the matter back to individual states to hash out. The aftermath was a swell of uncertainty and tension.

Fast-forward to June 2023, and over half the states have banned abortion outright, while others have severely restricted access to the procedure. In the meantime, legal fights are breaking out in courtrooms nationwide, quarreling over whether these new laws can be enforced.

Within the heart of this debate lies a fundamental division: the pro-life and pro-choice factions. Pro-life advocates, underpinned by a desire to protect what they see as emerging life, clash with pro-choice supporters, who champion a woman's right to autonomy over her own body. The moral and philosophical grounds on which this debate stands are as varied as the opinions themselves.

The religious context cannot be understated as it significantly influences the abortion discourse in America, a predominantly Christian nation. Many pro-life supporters ground their beliefs in the notion that human life begins at conception, weaving their spiritual beliefs with their political and social stances. Comparably, many traditional Buddhist scholars also believe that life begins at conception, although a deeper look at the EBTs reveals that the Buddha's teachings on consciousness and rebirth do not draw clear lines on this issue. Such ambiguity has led to more nuanced views on abortion among modern scholars, with some proposing that the moral status of the fetus depends on its level of consciousness and the mother's intentions.

Exploring the Buddha's Perspective on the Beginning of Life

In certain Buddhist communities, the belief that life starts at conception is often based on two suttas, one of which unfolds as an intriguing tale of a student challenging the Buddha on the question of caste. In response, the Buddha shares a story about seven Brahmin seers convinced of their superiority over other castes. They're so confident of their supremacy that they curse a dark-skinned seer named Devala, but their curses have no effect. Devala then asks them a series of questions to see if they know for sure whether their own ancestors were all Brahmins. The seers are unable to answer.

Next, Devala asks, "Do you know how an embryo is conceived?"

The seers respond in the affirmative, stating that conception occurs when a mother and father unite, the mother is in the fertile phase of her menstrual cycle, and the *gandhabba* is present.

In Buddhist cosmology, a gandhabba is a celestial being associated with music, dance, and fertility. In Hindu texts, the gandhabbas serve as attendants of Indra, the king of the gods. However, in this context, the prevalent understanding is that a gandhabba represents a stream of consciousness ready to be reborn into a human body. This interpretation draws from various texts and teachings that discuss the mechanics of rebirth and the continuity of consciousness.

Devala further asks, "But do you know for sure whether that gandhabba is an aristocrat, a Brahmin, a peasant, or a menial?"

"We don't know that," the seers confess.

At this juncture, the Buddha dismisses the Brahmin seers' claims of purity and superiority. He tells the student that claiming purity and supremacy over others is futile if, like the Brahmins in the story, one remains ignorant about their ancestors.

While the moral of this teaching is clear, another key takeaway lies in the fact that this tale of conception comes from Hindu thought. The entire discussion transpired between Devala, a Hindu sage, and seven Brahmin seers, without a single Buddhist participant.[1]

Interestingly, this theory of conception—the union of mother and father, fertility, and rebirth consciousness—appears again in another sutta, this time credited to the Buddha. However, it assumes a supporting role in an extensive discourse on dependent origination. It seems casually mentioned, along with a brief reference to a mother nurturing her embryo for nine months, to lend more credibility to this concept of conception.[2]

As we leap a few centuries ahead, we find that the belief that life begins when procreation meets the rebirth consciousness has interwoven itself into the fabric of various Buddhist schools. The Theravāda school advocates for an immediate intermediate rebirth, while the Mahāyāna school proposes a transitional phase, a sort of waiting room for up to forty-nine days before the rebirth consciousness takes a leap into the womb. This is why Mahāyāna followers observe a mourning period of forty-nine days when someone passes away, offering prayers every seven days for seven weeks. They believe these prayers support the departed in their journey to the next life.

In contrast, through the lens of several suttas, the Buddha presents life as a responsive, sentient existence. The transition from one life to the next is not a metaphysical passage but a tangible process that begins with the first stirrings of awareness within the womb. The Buddha teaches that life begins when a fetus becomes responsive to external stimuli, signaling the awakening of conscious life. A sentient being is an entity that "clings to desire, greed, relishing, and craving for the various aspects of existence."[3] This being is a complex weave of form, feeling, perception, choices, and consciousness, also known as the five aggregates. As described in the *Vajirā Sutta*, "When the parts are assembled, we use the word 'chariot.' So too, when the aggregates are present, 'sentient being' is the convention we use."[4]

The Buddha teaches that consciousness is a pivotal element for a future life to emerge,[5] while form provides a nurturing structure for consciousness to thrive.[6] Here, "form" signifies the neural networks in our brain that foster conscious experiences and any physical structures that aid the development of a fetus's mind within the womb. Once consciousness takes root, the fetus starts to desire, relish, and crave, much like a young sapling stretching toward the nourishing sunlight.[7]

Once, the Buddha poses two hypothetical questions to Ānanda to demonstrate the interaction of consciousness and "name and form": Would name and form manifest if consciousness wasn't conceived in the mother's womb? Moreover, if, after conception, consciousness was to be lost, could name and form still materialize in this world? Ānanda's negative response to both questions suggests that without consciousness, name and form cannot materialize; hence, no sentient being can come into being.[8]

This dialogue underscores the Buddha's belief that consciousness is an essential catalyst for the emergence of a sentient being. Without consciousness, the fusion of mental and physical phenomena (i.e., "name and form") could not manifest.

Drawing from these teachings, the beginning of life is a harmonious dance between mental and physical aspects, with consciousness taking the center stage. This suggests that a conscious fetus can feel pain and thus deserves moral consideration.

Scientific research indicates that around the six-month mark, a fetus's senses begin to connect with the brain. This milestone suggests that the fetus is not just a bundle of cells but is progressing toward a state of sentience, where it can interact with its environment in a more complex way. Therefore, abortion carried out before this six-month period may not be seen as taking the life of a "sentient being." However, it does raise ethical questions about overlooking the preservation of potential life, a decision not to be taken lightly.

Buddhism regards the birth of a human being as a precious and rare opportunity.[9] Hence, the Buddha would likely have advised people to think before they act—to prevent unwanted pregnancies in the first place by using protection, birth control, or other methods. But the Buddha would also have recognized that life is a complicated mess of nuances and shades of gray. Accidents happen, people are pushed into unwanted situations, and choices must be made. If a woman opts for an abortion due to financial reasons, health reasons, age, rape, incest, or a desire to pursue education or career advancement, the Buddha would have empathized with her situation.

Consider this fact from the US Center for Disease Control: an astonishing 93 percent of abortions happen within the first thirteen weeks. At this stage, the fetus is the size of a plum and weighs no more than twenty-five paperclips. It cannot feel pain.

But who bears the greatest pain and burden throughout the pregnancy?

Women.

Whether they decide to carry on with the pregnancy or opt for an abortion, women shoulder a heavy load. This decision, whatever it may be, often ushers in a storm of emotional turmoil and physical discomfort.

Through the lens of Buddhist feminism, the question isn't whether or not abortion should be legal but about how we can offer emotional, physical, and financial support to women who face this difficult and heart-wrenching decision.

As we ponder this, it's important to acknowledge the individual agency at play. Decisions of this magnitude often invite the scrutiny of our loved ones and stir internal conflicts rooted in our spiritual or cultural frameworks. Yet the Buddha instructs us, "Be an island unto yourself. Be your own refuge, with no other refuge."[10] He emphasizes that being controlled by others is suffering while being in control of ourselves is liberating.[11] We may be interconnected with family, friends, and broader society, but these relationships should serve to uplift us, not limit us. Should these bonds waver in their support, it falls on us to tap into our reservoir of inner strength. Ultimately, we are the ones most invested in our welfare, the only ones who fully grasp our deepest yearnings and dreams.

The Buddha declares, "I have no little hut. I have no nest. I have no networks. I'm free from shackles."[12] His words serve as a powerful reminder that we, too, can break free from any chains that restrict us. Like the Buddha, we possess the innate strength to rise above circumstances, find our voice, and make decisions that are right for us—ensuring our dignity, freedom, and well-being.

5

The Quest toward Gender Equality in Buddhism

In *An Arrow Sutta*, the Buddha offers a thought-provoking lesson on the nature of pain and suffering. He teaches that both physical and mental pain are part of life, but how we respond to these experiences sets apart the learned from the unlearned. A wise disciple remains resilient, skillfully evading the piercing sting of the second arrow, while the inexperienced endure both physical torment and mental distress.

This teaching has inspired the popular saying that "pain is inevitable, but suffering is optional." Yet when considering the experiences of women in Buddhism, this saying proves easier said than lived. Imagine not just two arrows but a downpour of arrows, each one sinking into the hearts of countless women navigating the stormy seas of Buddhism.

The first arrow strikes with the suggestion that buddhahood is a lofty, unreachable dream for women. Subsequent arrows come as misogynist narratives found in the Pāli Canon and other Buddhist texts. Then arrive the arrows of patriarchal structures and rules that favor men, societal barriers that hinder women's growth and aspirations, exclusion from Buddhist councils, silence in scriptural authorship, restricted access to full ordination, and a lack of societal support. These, coupled with the absence of basic respect and leadership representation, relentlessly test women's resilience, dignity, and faith.

Though women have become adept at adapting and crafting creative defenses against these challenges, this struggle is not theirs to face alone. Progress has been slow, and we are tired.

To help women extract these arrows until all that remains is a whisper of past pain, we need the entire Buddhist community, regardless of gender, to stand up for equity. Every voice that joins this cause accelerates our journey toward a more equal spiritual landscape.

As we rally our community, it's important to acknowledge an uncomfortable truth: despite the tireless efforts of advocates across the globe, some within Buddhist communities opt for deliberate ignorance or selective interpretation of the dharma. Far from heeding the Buddha's enduring principles of equality and nondiscrimination, these individuals perpetuate the view that women are inferior and unfit for certain roles. Such views are not just personal biases; they often manifest in the deliberate manipulation of texts, the reinforcement of monastic misogyny, and the perpetuation of institutional androcentrism.

It would be unfair, however, to presume malicious intent to all these monks without further inquiry. Some monks, consciously or unconsciously, cling to existing imbalances out of a misplaced sense of tradition or an unconscious fear of change. These views are often reinforced by religious texts that confirm these biases, creating an "echo chamber" where misogynist views are continually reaffirmed.

But the time to rectify this is now.

Envision a Buddhist world where women not only have equal opportunities and freedoms as men but also receive the support necessary to develop their spiritual capabilities to their fullest potential. Such a vision requires us to confront and challenge the status quo, to expose and correct the sexist bias that pervades many Buddhist texts, and to work toward more inclusive and equitable Buddhist communities.

In this chapter, we'll spotlight one arrow that has significantly hindered women's spiritual progress: the eight garudhammas, or "rules of respect." Later, in chapters 13 and 14, we'll dive into two more arrows: the Prātimokṣha, or "monastic code," and the deeply ingrained idea that monks alone are the rightful heirs to Buddhism. To wrap up this chapter, we'll outline tangible actions that every individual and organization can take to reverse centuries of systemic gender discrimination within Buddhism.

The Eight Rules of Respect

Let's start our journey with the tale of the first nun ordination, as detailed in the *Gotamī Sutta* and other Buddhist texts. This story has been passed down for centuries like a whispered secret: it vaguely resonates with us, yet rarely is it spoken of openly. Some scholars believe it's a myth to maintain the patriarchal hierarchy. Others believe it's a positive reminder that women have always been a part of this tradition and that they could achieve enlightenment, as affirmed by the Buddha himself. In any case, nearly all Buddhists, including many eminent monastics, regard it as a true, historical event.

The story unfolded at a time when the Buddha's father had just passed away. Mahāpajāpatī Gotamī, his foster mother, summoned the courage to approach the Buddha for ordination. He denied her request—three times.

Undeterred, Gotamī shaved her head, put on a saffron robe, and led a group of Sakyan women to Vesālī, where the Buddha was residing. There, dust-covered, exhausted, and with tears streaking her face, she waited outside the gates, hoping for help until Ānanda intervened on her behalf.

Ānanda repeated her plea three times to the Buddha, but each time he was met with the same answer: no. So Ānanda tried a different tactic. "Can women reach enlightenment?" he asked. The Buddha affirmed they could.

"Then sir," Ānanda said, "Gotamī has been very helpful to the Buddha. She is his aunt who raised and nurtured him, and fed him with her own milk when his birth mother died. Therefore, sir, please allow women to abandon their lay life and go forth in the teaching and training of the Realized One."

"If Gotamī agrees to abide by these eight rules of respect, that will be her ordination," the Buddha replied:

1. A nun, regardless of her years in the sangha, must prostrate herself before a newly ordained monk.
2. A nun cannot reside in a monastery during the rainy season without monks.
3. Twice a month, nuns should ask monks for advice and the date of the Sabbath.
4. After the rainy season, nuns should seek admonition from both monks and nuns concerning anything seen, heard, or suspected.
5. A nun who commits a grave offense must undergo penance before both monks and nuns for two weeks.

6. A trainee nun should ask to be ordained by both monks and nuns after two years.
7. A nun should never verbally abuse or insult a monk.
8. Nuns cannot criticize monks, but monks can criticize nuns.

With bated breath, Ānanda relayed the Buddha's conditions to Gotamī. Demonstrating her unwavering faith, Gotamī accepted them, earning her place in history as the first ordained Buddhist nun.

On the surface, this tale seems to reveal the Buddha's compassionate nature and his willingness to shatter tradition by formally institutionalizing a monastic path for women, a move almost unheard of at the time. Yet, this groundbreaking inclusion came bound with oppressive conditions that echoed the gender biases of the era. Furthermore, a deeper dive uncovers a trove of questionable implications, puzzling contradictions, and some aspects that might cause an eye roll.

One thing all Buddhists agree on is that the Buddha's father, King Suddhodhana, passed away around the fifth year of the Buddha's ministry, aged in his mideighties. If we accept the narrative of Gotamī's ordination, this implies that the inception of the nuns' order must have happened within the same year. However, according to the Vinaya Piṭaka—the first basket of the Pāli Canon, which serves as the foundational code of monastic discipline—the Buddha didn't lay down any rules for the first twenty years of his ministry. His early disciples were highly advanced monastics who behaved accordingly.

When Sāriputta suggested that the Buddha formulate some rules to ensure the spiritual life lasts a long time, the Buddha said that he wouldn't set down any rules until the causes of corruption appear in the sangha.[1] Moreover, he only crafted rules one at a time as specific situations came up.[2] So how could he suddenly produce eight rules for nuns, who hadn't engaged in any corrupt behavior?

Here's another chronological hiccup: at the time of the alleged ordination, Ānanda wasn't even a monk yet. According to one of the three surviving Vinaya lineages, Ānanda was born when the Buddha reached enlightenment. So he would've been five years old when Gotamī requested ordination. Even if we accept the Pāli Canon's claim that Ānanda was born on the same day as the Buddha, there's evidence in the Pāli Canon itself that Ānanda didn't become a monk until fifteen years after the nuns' order was established.

Let's look at a verse attributed to Ānanda, where he mentions being a trainee for twenty-five years around the time of the Buddha's death. If the Buddha died at eighty and Ānanda was a monk for twenty-five years, then he must've become a monk when the Buddha was about fifty-five, which was the twentieth year of the Buddha's ministry:

> When your friend has passed away,
> and your teacher is past and gone,
> there's no friend like
> mindfulness of the body.
> In the twenty-five years that have passed
> since I became a trainee,
> no sensual perception has arisen in me:
> see the excellence of the teaching!
> In the twenty-five years

since I became a trainee,
no malicious perception has arisen in me:
see the excellence of the teaching![3]

This verse suggests that Ānanda was significantly younger than the Buddha, which seems far more plausible. Would a spiritual leader with thousands of disciples prefer an attendant of the same age to care for him for twenty-five years, from the time they're both fifty-five until eighty?

According to the EBTs, Ānanda's attendant duties were far from glamorous. He was tasked with fetching water for the Buddha to wash his face, arranging seats for him, fanning him, keeping his room in order, and mending his robes. One might wonder if the Buddha, the embodiment of compassion, could have genuinely asked an elderly disciple to perform these mundane tasks for him every single day.

Even the Buddha himself suggested that Ānanda was younger. Once, when the Buddha was ill and Ānanda expressed his concern, the Buddha reminded him that he was "eighty years old, advanced in years, and have reached the final stage of life."[4] He then advised Ānanda to rely on himself and the teachings as his refuge after his passing.

Here's another intriguing inconsistency. If Ānanda became a monk at or before the establishment of the nuns' order, he would have been a monk for at least forty years when the Buddha passed into parinirvāṇa. With such extensive experience, he would likely be one of the most senior disciples and potentially the most revered. His esteem would not only come from his role as the Buddha's longest-serving and most trusted attendant but also from his unparalleled ability to retain the Buddha's teachings. In fact, Ānanda is universally recognized as the treasurer of the dharma and the founder of the entire canonical sutta tradition.

Yet, at the first communal recitation of the Buddha's teachings at Rājagaha—known as the First Buddhist Council—Ānanda almost wasn't allowed to join. He was still considered an "unenlightened trainee." Miraculously, he managed to attain enlightenment just before the council started and was allowed to participate. Still, during this gathering, he was admonished by various senior monks for five transgressions. These included not asking the Buddha which minor training rules could be abolished, accidentally stepping on the Buddha's rainy-season robe while sewing it, letting women pay their respects to the Buddha's deceased body first, failing to ask the Buddha to "live on for an eon for the benefit and happiness of humanity," and advocating for the ordination of women. Poor Ānanda had to confess his "wrong conduct" and apologize for each offense in front of 499 "enlightened monks."[5]

Can you picture that? Ānanda standing there, under the collective scrutiny of all those who claim enlightenment, subjected to a barrage of criticism and compelled to atone for actions they deemed wrong. Could this really be the atmosphere among the spiritually awakened?

Most Buddhist scholars question whether the first council happened. Personally, I'm convinced it's more fiction than fact. Storytellers are notorious for layering one exaggerated story on another to lend credibility to their narratives. First, they crafted the tale of Gotamī, and then they constructed the account of the First Buddhist Council. Each tale steeped in embellishment, leaving behind a trail of inconsistencies and outright falsities.

These manufactured stories lead us to two unsettling implications about the Buddha. First, they imply that Ānanda demonstrated greater compassion toward women, particularly toward the Buddha's own stepmother, than the Buddha himself did. Second, they paint a picture of the Buddha denying his stepmother's request for ordination not once, not twice, but an astonishing six times. Three from Gotamī. Three from Ānanda. Ultimately, it took Ānanda's clever reasoning to change the Buddha's mind.

Given this portrayal, we're led to question its authenticity. Can we reconcile this representation of the Buddha—who appears to lack filial piety, shows inadequate compassion toward women, and is outsmarted by Ānanda—with the image of the Buddha in the EBTs?

The Buddha teaches that caring for our parents is one of the highest blessings[6] and that their kindness is something we could never fully repay. As he once stated,

> You would not have done enough to repay your mother and father even if you were to carry your mother on one shoulder and your father on the other for a hundred years. Why is that? Parents are very helpful to their children: they raise them, nurture them, and show them the world. But you have done enough, more than enough, to repay them if you encourage, settle, and ground unfaithful parents in faith, unethical parents in ethical conduct, stingy parents in generosity, or ignorant parents in wisdom.[7]

According to this teaching, the best way to show our parents gratitude is to guide them toward a life filled with faith, ethics, generosity, and wisdom. Yet when his stepmother sought to embark on a spiritual journey to cultivate these very virtues, the Buddha is said to have refused her.

Elsewhere in the EBTs, the Buddha urges us to "honor, respect, esteem, and venerate" our parents,[8] to support them,[9] serve them,[10] care for them,[11] look after them,[12] and to be wise, respectful, and kindhearted for our parents' benefit, welfare, and happiness.[13] He declares, "Parents are our first teachers. They are kind to their children. They are worthy of offerings. Therefore, an astute person would revere them and honor them."[14]

Now, let's examine the *Gotamī Sutta* more closely. According to this text, after Gotamī was ordained, the Buddha told Ānanda that had women not been allowed to go forth, his teachings would have lasted a thousand years. But with women now joining the monastic fold, we're looking at only five hundred years. To illustrate his point, the Buddha drew three comparisons:

> Imagine families with many women and few men. They're easy prey for bandits and thieves. . . . Think of a field full of rice hit by the "white bones" disease. That crop won't last long. . . . Picture a sugarcane field attacked by a disease called "red rot." The same fate awaits. As a man might build a dike around a large lake as a precaution against the water overflowing, in the same way as a precaution, I've prescribed the eight rules of respect as not to be transgressed so long as life lasts.

The Buddha, a figure known for his compassion and wisdom, equated the inclusion of women in the monastic order—his own stepmother among them—to crimes, diseases, and natural disasters. These eight rules, in his eyes, were the floodgates holding back such calamities. The sutta, however, abruptly ends there, leaving the reasons for these severe comparisons cloaked in mystery.

One theory points to the societal norms of ancient India. Women were considered inferior to men and were often denied basic rights and freedoms. Given these conditions, it's conceivable that the Buddha in this tale worried that the sangha would lose respect and support from the local community for including women.

Buddhist texts also sometimes paint women as seductive—which in actuality is a projection from men and a deliberate attempt to depict women as inherently flawed. In any case, the Buddha in this tale might have been concerned about monks being led astray by nuns.

However, if we assume for one moment that these concerns preoccupied the Buddha's mind, the Buddha of the Gotamī tale seems to contradict the enlightened sage depicted across other sections of the EBTs. This Buddha would have viewed women as victims of societal biases and injustices, not as the instigators. He teaches that the world operates as a matrix of interconnections, emphasizing that there's no single cause for any issue and that ignorance, greed, and hatred are the root causes of all our problems.[15]

Moreover, he encourages his followers to collect their thoughts inward, much like a tortoise retracting its limbs into its shell. He advises us to be independent and to avoid disturbing others or blaming anyone.[16] Don't find fault with others, regardless of what they've done or left undone. Instead, focus on ourselves and our own actions.[17] In light of these teachings, attributing blame—particularly toward women—for the perceived decline of Buddhism would be fundamentally at odds with his core principles.

Consider, also, the Buddha's well-documented fearlessness. As a "fearless" spiritual leader,[18] he assures that those who are awake, mindful, and aware, brimming with joy and clarity, "have nothing to fear."[19] He emphasizes that "mastering and prevailing over fear and dread" is one of the eight qualities worthy of offerings and veneration.[20] He further posits that sorrow and fear spring from desire; therefore, one free from desire experiences no sorrow, let alone fear.[21]

Given this, it would seem paradoxical for such a fearless spiritual leader to be concerned about losing community support, monks being led astray by nuns or the endurance of his teachings.

The historical record also challenges this narrative of fragility. Around the fifth year of his ministry, the Buddha's teachings spread extensively like wildfire across India. He successfully converted several kings and kingdoms. By the time of his death, eight of sixteen kingdoms—nearly half of India—had embraced his teachings. The sangha, under his leadership, flourished. It always received ample support and respect from the community, even with the inclusion of nuns.

In his insightful work *White Bones Red Rot Black Snakes,* the venerable Australian monk Bhante Sujato observed that the grim prophecy of the dharma's decline and Buddhism's eventual downfall reflects the fear that permeated the Buddhist community during periods of uncertainty.

Following the Buddha's passing, Buddhism faced many challenges. Moral and ethical integrity within the sangha was eroding, while the growing antagonism of Brāhmaṇical-Hindu kings threatened to strip away royal support. Meanwhile, the emergence of new Buddhist schools stirred discord and fragmentation within the community. These unsettling shifts, further exacerbated by violent onslaughts from Arab and Turkish invaders nudged Buddhism into a phase of decline, casting long, worrisome shadows over the faith.

In the midst of this tumult, the community needed a fall guy—or, rather, fall gals.

Enter the nuns.

Bhante Sujato asks, "Who are we to blame?" He points out that the act of scapegoating is a long-standing human practice. Place the blame on others; let them shoulder the burden. In this case, the nuns became the scapegoat for Buddhism's impending downfall.

But as you may be aware, Buddhism did not meet its prophesied demise. It has endured for over 2,500 years and counting.

This raises another point: the Gotamī tale not only misrepresented the Buddha as lacking empathy for women, being unfilial to his stepmother, and anxiously doubting the resilience of his own teachings but also questioned his predictive wisdom. Those who crafted this tale—ironically some of the Buddha's most esteemed disciples—were willing to risk the integrity of their faith and tarnish the reputation of their teacher, all to deflect blame and maintain their social standing.

Remarkably, this strategy of deflection worked. It continues to work.

In some contemporary discussions about the challenges Buddhism has faced, the Gotamī tale is occasionally cited as a justification for placing restrictions on nuns. The tale has led to a persistent but contentious belief that the unregulated ordination of nuns could jeopardize the longevity of the dharma. This concern is mirrored in modern practices where, in some Buddhist lineages, women are denied full ordination. Furthermore, the eight rules of respect have institutionalized the secondary status of women in Buddhist monasteries. Yet if we dig into the EBTs, we find that in nearly three dozen discourses, the Buddha never singles out women, nuns, or gender as the root of any downfall. Instead, he's all about the conduct of individuals—their discipline, their character.[22]

The Buddha teaches that the true dharma fades when his followers don't listen, remember, implement the teachings, or ponder the deeper meaning.[23] Decline happens when we lack respect and reverence for the dharma, the sangha, the training, diligence, and hospitality.[24]

Other factors contributing to the decline include exhibiting negligence and laziness, having many wishes, lacking contentment, lacking situational awareness, not paying attention, associating with the wrong crowd, and adopting harmful habits.[25]

Near the end of his life, the Buddha laid out forty-one guidelines to prevent any decline in the sangha. And there was not a single reference to gender or nuns. There was none of that gender bias that made its way into the Gotamī tale.

Imagine a past where monks not only refrained from marginalizing women but also followed the Buddha's teachings on the "six warm-hearted qualities."[26] These monks would consistently treat all their spiritual companions with bodily, verbal, and mental kindness, both in public and in private. This genuine warmth would cultivate an environment of fondness and respect conducive to inclusion, harmony, and unity rather than division. Such monks would also generously share their material possessions, even the food in their alms bowls. Living in accordance with noble views that lead to the end of suffering, they would create a sangha that is not just unified but deeply committed to the path of enlightenment. With such a foundation, can we not envision a present-day Buddhism that is not only more inclusive and progressive but also profoundly impactful, extending its reach far beyond its current scope?

The Buddha encourages his disciples to live in such a way so that "more good-hearted spiritual companions might come, and those that have already come may live comfortably."[27] This teaching sharply contrasts with his portrayal in the Gotamī tale, where he appears reluctant to admit nuns into his sangha.

Moreover, the Buddha warns that those consumed by hostility, stinginess, jealousy, and deceit, with hearts full of desire, may lead to the downfall of the dharma.[28] In light of this teaching, might it be that the monks who penned the Gotamī tale—by attempting to belittle, control, and exclude women—were actually significant contributors to Buddhism's decline themselves? An unexpected twist, isn't it? All along, it was the monks, not the nuns, who kicked off the downward spiral.

Who wants to keep playing this finger-pointing game?

I do; let's keep going: the Buddha also speaks of a haunting vision of the dharma's decline—a time when monastics would be drawn to the words "composed by poets with fancy words and phrases, or by outsiders or spoken by disciples," thinking these teachings are worth learning and memorizing instead of his teachings.[29] Does this not eerily mirror how the Gotamī tale has entrenched itself within Buddhism?

The fact that this tale has survived through centuries and continues to shape Buddhist communities today is nothing short of mind-boggling.

Consider, for instance, the case of the esteemed Ajahn Sumedho, the first Western disciple of Ajahn Chah. In 2010, Ajahn Sumedho and his senior monks drafted the Five-Point Declaration, which solidified the position of monks above nuns in their monastic hierarchy. This divisive document has since cast long shadows over his community in England, making the spiritual path of female practitioners more challenging and unequal.

Jump to the present, and we're still wrestling with the echoes of these biases. Some nuns at Sumedho's monastery chose to stay, but many left. Two of the leavers founded a new community in the United States, and since then, many more women have taken full ordination as nuns.

Imagine having to relocate to a new country and build your own spiritual refuge just to pursue your spiritual aspirations. Why don't we see men having to do this? They get to stroll into any monastery, anywhere in the world, and receive ordination while expecting respect and dignity.

It's worth noting that while the Gotamī tale and other such controversial narratives make up less than 1 percent of the Pāli Canon, they offer a fascinating peek into the past, showing how the Buddha's teachings were molded by the world in which they emerged.

One thing is clear: the Gotamī tale and its eight rules reveal far more about their authors than those they sought to demean. These texts lay bare the insecurities, shamelessness, and narrow-mindedness of their creators, spotlighting how sacred texts can suffer distortions from patriarchy. They stand as glaring reminders of the male privilege and fragility that have long been interwoven into Buddhism's fabric. And despite being few and far between, it's these texts that some people cherry-pick today to prevent women from fully participating in Buddhism worldwide, from Asia to America and everywhere in between.

This state of affairs cannot continue unchallenged. Until we collectively raise our voices and expose the Gotamī tale for what it truly is—a constructive narrative serving the interests of a patriarchal system—we are allowing these "eight rules of respect" to persist as barriers. These barriers not only hinder women from achieving spiritual equality but also impede our collective journey toward a more inclusive, compassionate, and enlightened practice.

Equity Is the Path If Equality Is the Goal

October 2022. Alongside my fellow pilgrims, I found myself at a Thai *wat* in Nautanwa, a peaceful interlude surrounded by towering trees and lush greenery. We were all poised on the brink of an adventure, awaiting our visas for Nepal, our spirits already soaring toward the ancient city of Lumbini, the birthplace of the Buddha.

A Thai monk, clothed in a saffron robe, welcomed us with a warm smile. He motioned toward a charming coffee and water station, enveloped by a brick walkway and stately trees. We couldn't walk to the station fast enough. Free coffee in the middle of the day? Yes, please!

As I strolled along the walkway, a steaming cup of coffee in hand, my attention was caught by the sight of a figure in a white robe—a Thai *maechi*, or partially ordained nun, engaged in an animated conversation with a local.

When their exchange drew to a close, I approached the maechi, eager to make a connection. She greeted me with a wide smile and a few Thai words. I shook my head apologetically. "I'm sorry, I don't understand."

Her eyes twinkled with understanding.

"May I take a picture with you?" I said, pointing at my phone.

Her nod was more enthusiastic this time.

As we snapped our photo and bid farewell, I hoped my smiles and nods conveyed my deep admiration for her commitment and the courage she displayed in the face of the often underestimated challenges that nuns within her tradition face.

In many cultures, the scene often unfolds like this: crowds are drawn toward the monks, under the belief that interactions or donations to them yield greater merit. It's as though our collective psyche has decided that the monks are the only spiritual guides we need, sidelining nuns and female practitioners, placing them at a disadvantage even before the race begins.

By acknowledging the maechi that day, I felt I'd made a teeny tiny stride against this trend. I didn't request a photo with the monk—I'm sure he was no stranger to such requests. But the maechi? I'd like to believe that, for that fleeting moment, she experienced a sense of visibility and dignity. Sometimes, that's all it takes—a glimmer of recognition. Former First Lady Michelle Obama captures this beautifully in *The Light We Carry*: "It's these small rearrangements that help us untangle the bigger knots." If each of us takes such small steps, we can unravel the twisted yarn of patriarchy, leading us to a brighter, kinder world.

At present, buzzwords like *gender equity* and *inclusivity* are mostly confined to academic papers or theoretical debates. Sure, most of us nod in agreement, but consensus about the roadmap to equity is far from universal. What we often see are token gestures. Organizations make that one diversity hire, run a handful of surveys, and maybe introduce a new policy aimed at minimizing harm.

It's high time we move beyond surface-level measures. True commitment demands integrating equity principles into the fabric of our daily existence. In the context of Buddhism, this means embarking on a thorough examination of our texts, rules, and norms—casting off biases and carving a clear route toward gender equality in every nook and cranny of our spiritual life.

How do we go about this exactly? Well, here's a cheat sheet of sorts.

Imagine a world where we rally behind women and nuns, providing financial, material, and emotional support. Where we partner with local sanghas and governments to boot out sexist laws. Where the establishment of nun sanghas across the globe is met with enthusiasm. Where nunneries multiply and nuns find open doors in traditionally male monasteries. Where nuns can erect their own monasteries, steering their own communities.

And we're just getting started.

What if women and nuns were given a voice in decision-making processes? What if domestic chores were shared by all in multifold sanghas? What if the well-being and spiritual growth of women were prioritized? What if women and nuns were not pushed into the shadows but placed in the spotlight at events and in public spaces? What if they were offered opportunities to share dharma talks, translate texts, and undertake meaningful monastic tasks?

Let's take it further.

We could launch educational campaigns to shatter sexist thinking and discrimination and reject any hint of male superiority. We could provide training to uncover and eliminate unconscious bias. We could strive to create environments where everyone feels valued and seen, from our temples to our meditation circles and online communities. We could engage in genuine dialogues with those who resist these changes, seeking common ground.

In my own journey, I've found most monks to be gracious, understanding, and open to change. But we've arrived at a crucial crossroads where patchwork solutions are insufficient. It's not enough to merely bandage the wounds; we need to heal the system from within. Should a Buddhist council convene in the future, I want to see nuns have equal seats at the table. I hope for a future where everyone, regardless of their background, walks side by side in our spiritual journey. If the Buddha could foster a thriving multifold sangha, we have the potential to do the same. It demands initiative, clarity, and a profound commitment to living the dharma, and we can do it.

Make no mistake: the future of Buddhism is one of gender equality. It's not a dream hovering in the clouds but a reality that needs to be grounded. It's not a game of tug-of-war but a win-win situation. The moment we tear down barriers holding women back, we unleash a tidal wave of talent, creativity, passion, and productivity that uplifts us all.

As we near the end of this chapter, I find my thoughts drifting to my nieces, Aurora and Aria, their faces lit up with dreams that are still taking shape, much like the clouds on a breezy day.

Aurora, on her first day of first grade, holding a blackboard etched with her name and her dream of becoming a veterinarian. Aria echoed her sister's ambitions with a sparkle in her eyes. "I want to be a vet too," she said.

Their joy, their zeal—they are infectious, a reminder of the infinite possibilities the future holds. As their aunt, I see it as both a privilege and a responsibility to keep the doors of opportunity wide open for them, to nurture their self-belief, guiding them to pursue their aspirations, goals, or life missions, wherever they might lead.

I dream of a day when my nieces, and all girls and women everywhere, will ascend beyond the shackles of societal norms and expectations. They will define themselves not by their gender, age, or past but by their dreams, actions, and the love they radiate. They will not only cross the threshold of opportunity but will hold it wide open for others. They will chart their own paths, amplify their truths, and follow their hearts. In their unique and resplendent ways, they will rise, leaving an indelible imprint on the world.

American Buddhism

6

Why Buddhism Is *Mostly* True—Sorry, Robert Wright

I lifted my eyes from the fragrant bowl of rice and lemongrass chili mushrooms before me, meeting my parents' gaze across the dining table. "Ba Má, I don't want to go to the temple anymore," I said, trying to keep any trace of hesitation out of my voice.

My father's firm yet understanding eyes met mine. He nodded, his voice steady, "Alright. If you don't want to go, you don't have to."

My mother, too, gave her silent consent with a gentle nod.

A relieved *thank you* escaped my lips, followed by the clinking of chopsticks against the white porcelain bowl.

The year was 1998. I was twelve, in a country far from my birthplace, and each day felt like exploring a cosmos of opportunities. Two years into our American journey, I was still in awe of the towering skyscrapers, the sheer abundance of everything from food to clothing to gadgets, and the nonstop, high-energy vibe of this foreign land. Among learning English, making new friends, dribbling basketballs, and catching up on *Rugrats*, *The*

Simpsons, and *Whose Line Is It Anyway?*, spirituality seemed like a faint echo in the symphony of this new life.

On top of that, our small Pure Land temple in Northeast Olympia, a modest bungalow adorned with a few Buddhist flags and crowned by a serene white Quan Âm statue overlooking a small lotus pond was far from the majestic temples back in Việt Nam. To a great extent, it was a mirror, reflecting the journey of Vietnamese immigrants—a story of struggle, adaptation, and resilience.

In the early years of my American life, Buddhism was a mere whisper in the nation's collective consciousness. Vietnamese Buddhism felt like a fragile, delicate flame trying to stay alight in the gusty winds of an unfamiliar landscape.

The temple was far from abundant, lacking in resources, structure, and programming for youths and adults. There was only one elderly monk in residence, and I can't recall him ever speaking to me or offering any dharma talks. The adult chanting sessions were conducted in transcriptions of classical Chinese. While their rhythmic flow had a soothing effect, I couldn't understand the words or grasp how they were helping me become a better Buddhist, let alone a better person.

It wasn't until a college study-abroad trip to Việt Nam in 2007 that my spiritual curiosity was rekindled. The deep tranquility of the monasteries and a chance meeting with a junior monk at Từ Đàm Pagoda left a lasting impression on me. The monk was visibly younger than me, yet he spoke in a soft, gentle voice. He walked me through the temple, his quiet wisdom about Buddhism shining from him like the soft glow of a nightlight. That meeting sparked a tiny flame of peace and inspiration in me, a flame I've carried back to America and have been carefully tending ever since.

But instead of going back to the Olympia temple, I began practicing Buddhism on my own. I delved into Buddhist texts, listened to online dharma talks, and attended retreats across various schools, including Vietnamese Zen, Korean Seon, Japanese Zen, Sakya Tibetan, Thai Forest, and Burmese vipassanā.

This spiritual quest led me to the Plum Village Zen Tradition, founded by Zen Master Thích Nhất Hạnh. After a three-year immersion in this practice, I cofounded Cherry Blossom Sangha in Seattle. Our sangha's guiding principles embodied ideals like nurturing joy, peace, and wisdom, welcoming people from all spiritual and cultural backgrounds, viewing no one as superior, inferior, or the same as any other members, and promoting a positive spirit of friendship, understanding, and harmony.

Around this time, my family dubbed me the "Buddhist enthusiast" of the house. The hum of dharma talks replaced the latest billboard hits on my car rides. I couldn't help but share Buddhist wisdom with my family at every opportunity, much to their amusement and occasional annoyance. I even purchased a brown Buddhist robe and mused with my younger sister about what kind of reaction I'd get if I wore it for a casual walk around Green Lake, a popular destination for recreation in Seattle.

"Go for it," she said. "I'll come with you."

"Really?"

"Yeah. I'll bring my phone. Snap a few photos for the memory book."

While I never ended up wearing the robe for our Green Lake adventure, the Buddha's call to swim upstream was like a fire in my soul, burning away my doubts and fears. Society often tempts us toward happiness through beauty, wealth, and fame. But the Buddha? His message is more like "True happiness comes from within. Tune out the noise. Master your mind.

Embrace peace, acceptance, and contentment. Do what makes your heart sing." And if wearing a brown robe makes my heart sing, why not?

My decision to leave the robe behind wasn't due to fear of public perception but from the realization that my still fully haired head might raise more eyebrows than inspire others. Many of the things I was doing at the time—facilitating Cherry Blossom Sangha gatherings, serving on nonprofit boards, emceeing at charity events—were my attempts to kindle positive change, not just in my life but in society as a whole. The sense of purpose and fulfillment I derived from this was deeply gratifying.

This understanding prompted me toward a life-altering decision in 2017. I bid farewell to my role as a citizenship program specialist for the City of Seattle and embarked on a residential internship at a Vietnamese Zen monastery in El Paso, dreaming of eventually donning the brown robe for real as a Buddhist nun. But my time there revealed the hidden shadows lurking within spiritual communities, including the harmful echoes of patriarchal and hierarchical systems.

If there's one gem I've discovered from my journey so far, it's this: Our spiritual path is a living, breathing entity, evolving as we learn and grow. It's not set in the stars nor bound by the tradition of our birth. It's perfectly okay, even necessary, to change course if it no longer aligns with our beliefs. We have the power to shape our spiritual journey, to seek out spaces that resonate with our unique quests. And if such spaces don't exist, we might need to take matters into our own hands and create them ourselves.

As I ventured deeper into Buddhism, I noticed a conspicuous absence: an Indigenous American Buddhist monastic community. While American monastics practiced Buddhism within imported traditions, a genuinely homegrown American monasticism was missing.

But this absence isn't a void—it's fertile ground for possibilities. Buddhism in America is still a budding lotus, waiting to unfurl its petals. As Buddhism adapts to the cultural and societal norms of the countries it reaches, America has the potential to cultivate a unique interpretation of Buddhism that reflects its rich ideals of democracy, equality, opportunity, and freedom.

Wandering off the Main Trails

Imagine a treasure hunter—let's call her Chloe—armed with Robert Wright's celebrated bestseller *Why Buddhism Is True* as her map. Eager to unlock the secrets of the mind, she follows the well-marked trails of mindfulness, impermanence, and the puzzling concept of not-self. Wright, candid about his omission of Buddhism's supernatural elements, serves as her trusted guide through a forest brimming with wisdom, asserting that modern science is the compass that validates these ancient teachings. But what if I told you that Chloe's map, while meticulously designed, reveals only the well-trodden expanses of the forest?

Wright's lens, while insightful, focuses mainly on Buddhism's foundational principles, steering clear of its mystical and cultural dimensions and the dense underbrush of historical biases, misogyny, and exclusionary perspectives. It's like taking a hike through a rich, complex forest but only sticking to the main trails. This brings us to an important consideration: the book's title is a marketing masterstroke, and we need to understand it as such—more a promotional lure than an unassailable truth.

If you've been on this journey with me from the start, you know we've already strayed from these beaten paths. We've scrutinized established narratives, beliefs, and practices that have deviated from the Buddha's message over time. As we delve further in the following pages, we'll confront more twists in the path—teachings and traditions that got muddled along the way—sometimes intentionally, sometimes not. Our exploration will challenge the authenticity of certain practices and ideologies within Buddhism's history, seeking to understand the complex reasons behind the development of these elements that continue to shape contemporary Buddhist thought.

This deep dive is not meant to undermine Buddhism but to sharpen our focus on its most liberating aspects—the parts that truly alleviate life's suffering, reflecting the core of the Buddha's message. It's my hope that through this process, we'll foster a discerning, questioning approach that critically examines Buddhist doctrines and practices rather than simply taking them on faith. In doing so, we pave the way for a continually evolving, vibrant, and inclusive American Buddhism—one that not only resonates but also amplifies the timeless wisdom of the Buddha, standing tall like the grandest tree in our ever-expanding forest of understanding.

From Siddhārtha to Modern Day

Our exploration commences with a young prince, Siddhārtha Gautama (*Siddhatta Gotama* in Pāli), who traded his life of luxury at the tender age of twenty-nine to seek the "supreme state of sublime peace."[1] Through relentless self-discipline and intense meditation, he reached enlightenment, emerging as the Buddha, or the "Awakened One." For the following forty-five years, he roamed across different lands, teaching the dharma—the path to liberation from suffering—and establishing the sangha, a monastic community.

In the wake of the Buddha's final breath around 410 BCE, his followers were concerned about preserving his teachings against the tides of change. It's said that a First Buddhist Council convened a mere three months after his passing to compile and recite his teachings. The Second Council? Fast-forward a century. The Third? Double that. The Fourth? Add another three centuries. The Fifth? Not until 2,000 years. And, finally, the Sixth Council convened 2,344 years after the Buddha's departure from this world, held between 1954 and 1956 in Myanmar.

Sources suggest that the sangha split into various schools around the Second Council, and whether some of these early councils took place or not continues to be a matter of debate among scholars. But one thing is certain: Despite the Buddha's vision of inclusive gatherings where everyone—monks, nuns, and laypeople—actively engaged in preserving and transmitting his teachings, these councils consisted solely of monks. Nuns and laypeople were neither invited nor allowed to participate.

The Buddha declares, "I have disciples who are competent monks and nuns, celibate laymen and laywomen, and laymen and laywomen enjoying sensual pleasures. You should all come together and recite what I've taught you, comparing meaning with meaning, and phrase with phrase, so that this spiritual path may last for a long time. That would be for the welfare and happiness of the people, out of compassion for the world."[2]

Yet somewhere along the line, this message of inclusivity got lost. And so this systematic discrimination resulted in a spiritual hierarchy that prevented nuns and laypeople from fully engaging with, learning, and contributing to Buddhism for over two thousand years.

But this penchant for exclusion and discrimination wasn't content with merely sidelining others at recitation councils—it also crept into the texts.

We've already dissected certain texts with misogynistic undertones in previous discussions, such as the *Gotamī Sutta*. Despite their scarcity within the 11,500 suttas that comprise the EBTs—specifically, the first four nikāyas: the Dīgha, Majjhima, Saṃyutta, and Aṅguttara, along with half of the Khuddaka Nikāya of the Sutta Piṭaka—the unsettling resonance of these texts is stark. For instance, consider a sutta that casts women in the same negative light as the "five drawbacks of a black snake," attributing to them qualities like irritability, hostility, sensuousness, deceit, and infidelity.[3]

And then there are the Mahāyāna sūtras—texts composed centuries after the Buddha's passing. Venturing into the realm of Mahāyāna sūtras can sometimes feel like stepping into a fantastical landscape of miraculous deeds and celestial beings. These texts introduce us to a host of new characters, themes, and concepts seldom encountered in the EBTs. Among these enchanting narratives, we also occasionally stumble on troubling passages that perpetuate harmful stereotypes and prejudices, especially concerning women.

A harsh example is the *Great Nirvāṇa Sūtra*, penned nearly five hundred years after the Buddha's passing. This text paints women with an unflattering brush, reducing our intricate selves to blunt statements such as "All good men and women desire to be born as a man. Why so? Because females are the nests of evil."

The *Great Nirvāṇa Sūtra* also tells a story about a wealthy man who is disheartened on learning that his wife is carrying a daughter. He approaches the Buddha, voicing his disappointment. The

Buddha in this tale, however, transforms his sorrow into joy, assuring him his unborn child will in fact be a virtuous son. And . . . that's it. That's the end of the story. Short, to the point, yet leaves a lasting impact on society. It promotes and reinforces a cultural preference for sons—a mindset that has permeated Asian societies for thousands of years and continues to linger today.

This bias was gently confronted in 2016 when President Barack Obama, on a state visit to Việt Nam, stopped by the Jade Emperor Pagoda—a Taoist temple established by a Chinese merchant in 1909. A resident monk suggested that Obama pray to a fertility goddess for a son. The president, already a proud father to Malia and Sasha, simply smiled and replied, "I like daughters."

Thank you, Obama, for succinctly turning a moment of traditional expectation on its head.

Let's now cast our gaze back to the third century BCE, to the era of Ashoka the Great. Ashoka's reign began with violence and bloodshed. In his early years as king, Ashoka led brutal wars that resulted in the loss of thousands of lives. But it was the Kalinga War, with its staggering death toll of around 100,000, that flipped a switch in Ashoka's heart. This brutal confrontation led him to embrace Buddhism, sparking a journey of social and religious reforms.

Ashoka began building hospitals and schools, promoting nonviolence and the Buddha's teachings, and encouraging tolerance of all religions. He even sent Buddhist ambassadors throughout his kingdom and beyond.

Among these ambassadors were his son, Mahinda, and his daughter, Saṅghamittā. They introduced Theravāda Buddhism to Sri Lanka. From Sri Lanka, Theravāda Buddhism expanded its reach across Southeast Asia, making its mark in countries like Myanmar, Thailand, Cambodia, Laos, and others.

Fast-forward to five hundred years after Ashoka's passing, and we find the Kushan Empire significantly influencing Buddhism's spread. The Gandhara region, located in present-day Pakistan, became a vibrant hub of Buddhist art and culture.

The Kushans propelled Buddhism into central Asia and China, fostering trade and cultural exchange. In China, Buddhism began to blend with local ideologies like Confucianism and Taoism, leading to the emergence of different Buddhist schools. The Pure Land school, Zen, and the Lotus school all sprang up during this period.

These schools added their unique twist to Buddhism, infusing it with new cosmological, theological, and philosophical perspectives. Collectively, they gave rise to Mahāyāna, a broad tradition that later took hold across East Asia and the Himalayas, flourishing in places like Việt Nam, Japan, Korea, Malaysia, Mongolia, Nepal, Tibet, and Bhutan.

Meanwhile, back in India, a new variation was taking place: Vajrayāna Buddhism, also known as Tantric Buddhism. This subsect of Mahāyāna introduced unique elements to Buddhist practice like mantras, mudras, and mandalas. By the seventh century, Vajrayāna made its way to Tibet, giving birth to new schools within Indo-Tibetan Buddhism such as the Nyingma, Kagyu, Sakya, and Gelug schools. Today, Vajrayāna resonates across Mongolia, Nepal, Bhutan, central Asia, and parts of modern-day Russia and China.

The Buddha's teachings, like a seed in the wind, are carried to all corners of the earth. A 2018 survey by the Pew Research Center estimated that Buddhism has amassed a following of around 506 million people, making it the fourth-largest religion worldwide.

Buddhism Takes Root in America

Buddhism has graced American shores for a little over 150 years. That's a mere ripple in the vast ocean of history. The journey began with Chinese immigrants bringing their faith to the American West Coast in the mid-nineteenth century. But the seeds of Buddhism didn't truly germinate and flourish in the soil of American culture until the twentieth century.

Eastern spirituality began to capture the American imagination, thanks in part to influential figures of the time. The Dalai Lama, with his humble wisdom and magnetic charm, became one of the spiritual superstars of the era, igniting the curiosity of non-Asian Americans about Buddhism.

The winds of World War II also carried the scent of Buddhism to America, with soldiers returning home carrying stories and teachings from the East.

The Beat Generation's fascination with Eastern philosophies, spotlighted by figures like Jack Kerouac, Alan Watts, and Gary Snyder further opened the door to Buddhism for a broader American audience. This led to the sprouting up of Buddhist centers and the emergence of homegrown American Buddhist teachers.

By the twenty-first century, Buddhism was no longer a hidden gem or an exotic mystery. From pop culture to sports to the digital sphere, it's hard to miss. Legendary NBA coach Phil Jackson and his star player, Michael Jordan, spoke about using Zen Buddhism principles to help them win championships.

Meditation and mindfulness apps popped up everywhere. Buddhist symbols like the lotus flower and the *om* symbol appeared in mainstream fashion and decor.

Surveys suggest that over thirty million people in the United States identify themselves as Buddhists, practice Buddhist spirituality without labeling themselves as religious, or have been strongly influenced by Buddhism.

7

The Future of American Buddhism

American Buddhism is woven from the diverse threads of various cultures, ethnicities, and traditions that make up the United States. Far from being a monolithic entity imported wholesale from the East, it has evolved into a dynamic practice uniquely tailored to the social and cultural landscape of America. This rich plurality within American Buddhism allows for a broad spectrum of interpretations and practices, making it accessible and relevant to people from all walks of life.

While chapter 11 will offer an in-depth look at other prominent schools of Buddhism in America—such as Theravāda, Mahāyāna, and Vajrayāna, as well as Indo-Tibetan traditions—this chapter focuses on a rising trend that particularly resonates with American converts and spiritual seekers: secular Buddhism.

In the same way that modern artists interpret traditional forms to create new works, secular Buddhism offers a recontextualization of the Buddha's teachings for the twenty-first century. This approach integrates Buddhism into everyday activities—sipping morning coffee, navigating through rush-hour traffic, or maintaining composure during a spirited debate. Distancing itself from the formality of rituals and the repetition of mystical chants, secular Buddhism strives for a practice that can be seamlessly incorporated into modern routines.

This revolution is led by individuals much like us—social workers, engineers, bookkeepers, those who form the cornerstone of our local fabric. Names such as Doug Smith, the creator of Doug's Dharma on YouTube, and Noah Rasheta, the host of the podcast *Secular Buddhism* are at the forefront, championing this accessible and practical interpretation of Buddhism.

Their efforts have paved the way for the widespread acceptance of vipassanā and mindfulness movements in America. These straightforward approaches to meditation and conscious living have found a place in the most unexpected corners—from the towering skyscrapers of corporate America to the buzzing classrooms of public schools and even within the silent confines of prisons. Stockbrokers find Zen amid high-stakes trades, teachers replace detention slips with moments of meditation, and prisoners seek solace in the rhythm of their breath rather than the length of their sentence.

A Modern Take on Ancient Wisdom

Vipassanā, or insight meditation, was rejuvenated by a group of devoted Theravāda monks from Myanmar. Their vision was to make meditation as commonplace as a morning walk. They simplified the practice to make it accessible to everyone, focusing on the breath or body sensations, a method that requires minimal training. This approach, often referred to as *pure* or *dry* insight, allows people with busy lives to practice without striving for the four blissful meditations, or jhānas[1]—joy, rapture, bliss, equanimity—within their current life.

In time, their teachings traveled across the globe, inspiring modern techniques such as Jon Kabat-Zinn's Mindfulness-Based Stress Reduction program and leading to the establishment of vipassanā centers like the Insight Meditation Society in Massachusetts.

In America today, vipassanā serves as a mental compass for many, guiding them through the ups and downs of life. It has become a tradition of seeing clearly into the true nature of reality through equanimous observation of bodily sensations. It encourages us to notice how things constantly change (impermanence), how life isn't always satisfying (suffering), and how our sense of "self" is not an isolated entity but a construct intricately linked to the larger universe (not-self). By becoming aware of these three marks of existence, we're taking the first steps toward stream entry—the first stage of awakening—eventually leading to complete liberation.

However, as much as vipassanā has been transformative for many grappling with stress, anxiety, and depression, it isn't without its shadows. Some scholars argue that vipassanā presents a personal interpretation of the Buddha's teachings, colored by later Buddhist texts. For example, the "sixteen insight knowledges" written by Buddhaghosa—a fifth-century Theravāda scholar—are often used as a yardstick to measure a practitioner's progress but are sometimes mistaken as a direct teaching of the Buddha.

Along the same line, the Abhidhamma—a collection of Buddhist psychological and philosophical teachings traditionally said to have been organized and systematized several centuries after the Buddha's lifetime—and its commentaries tend to relegate samatha bhāvanā, or serenity meditation, to the sidelines, presenting it as merely a prelude to vipassanā. But, according to the Buddha, samatha and vipassanā aren't independent practices; they're the dynamic duo developing side by side as we walk the eightfold path.[2] Both practices are essential for a complete and well-rounded spiritual journey.

While the three marks of existence—impermanence, suffering, and not-self—form the foundation of vipassanā practice and are often intertwined in the EBTs, they're not an exclusive trio. The Buddha was fluid in his teachings, occasionally pairing impermanence and suffering with other concepts such as "perishable," "giving up," and "fading away."[3]

Moreover, there are many roads leading to stream entry beyond the three marks of existence. For instance, we could become a stream enterer by practicing the eightfold path,[4] by eliminating the three fetters (doubt, attachment to rites and rituals, and belief in self),[5] or through experiential confidence in the Three Jewels—Buddha, dharma, and sangha—coupled with ethical conduct.[6] The Buddha's teachings, like a map of the mind, offer multiple paths leading to the same center.

Then there's the whispering winds of the rumor mill, spread by some teachers who advocate vipassanā as the "one true path to liberation." All the while, the Buddha's well-established eightfold path remains the most time-honored roadmap to spiritual awakening.

The Buddha emphasizes the critical role of the eightfold path. He states that without its presence, one could not find a true monastic.[7] He declares, "Health is the ultimate blessing," and the highest form of happiness is "extinguishment," which, to be clear, doesn't involve any actual flames. Instead, it refers to the elimination of the root causes of suffering—greed, hatred, and delusion. It's essentially the peace train to nirvāṇa. And the first-class ticket to this destination? The eightfold path, the most reliable route to the "deathless."[8]

The term *deathless* in the Buddha's teachings denotes "the liberation of the mind" achieved through not grasping,[9] which is another descriptor for nirvāṇa.

It's worth mentioning that the eightfold path includes the four blissful meditations or absorptions, which, as mentioned earlier, vipassanā considers nonessential. In a teaching where the Buddha emphasizes the interdependence of serenity and insight meditations in the journey toward enlightenment, he specifically reminds us to "not neglect absorption."[10] In fact, absorption and wisdom are like two sides of the same coin. The Buddha declares, "No absorption for one without wisdom, no wisdom for one without absorption. But one with absorption and wisdom—they have truly drawn near to extinguishment."[11]

While vipassanā and mindfulness are having their moment in the spotlight in the West, let's not forget that the Buddha taught a diverse array of meditation techniques. These include the four ways of developing immersion,[13] the five elements of escape,[14] meditation on emptiness[15] and love,[16] and reflections on ethical conduct and generosity.[17] It's a long list, but you get the idea.

As vipassanā continues to make strides in American society, I believe adopting a balanced perspective is key—understanding its strengths and limitations, its potential for profound impact, and occasional oversights. By aligning vipassanā with the EBTs, we can uphold its fidelity to the original teachings of the Buddha. This alignment not only enriches vipassanā's transformative potential but also extends the promise of peace and mental clarity to all who seek it.

Mindfulness beyond the Hype

Like an age-old manuscript translated into a contemporary tongue, mindfulness has been secularized to a degree that, in many respects, has strayed from the Buddha's original teachings.

You may have stumbled upon descriptions of mindfulness that make it sound as effortless as microwaving popcorn. It's all about being in the present, refraining from judging our thoughts and feelings, simply letting them flow, right? That's the general impression you might get from sources like Wikipedia, Dictionary.com, and even some academic resources and Buddhist teachers. While this isn't entirely incorrect, these descriptions miss the depth and breadth of the practice. It's like saying an iPad is a device for media consumption—technically true but overlooks a whole lot of other features and functions.

According to the EBTs, the ultimate goal of practicing the four foundations of mindfulness is far-reaching: to purify oneself, to overcome sorrow, to cease suffering, to understand the nature of reality, and to realize liberation.[18]

The Buddha laid out a comprehensive guide.

For mindfulness of the body, he teaches us to tune in to our breathing, our postures, and our body's actions, elements, and contents, recognizing that all bodies share commonalities—they're born, they age, and they die.

For mindfulness of feelings, the Buddha teaches us to discern when we're feeling joy, sorrow, or neutrality and to understand whether we're experiencing physical pain or spiritual happiness. The goal is to stay attuned to our feelings without becoming entangled in worldly attachments.

Moving on to mindfulness of mind, the Buddha teaches us to understand the different mental states, whether they're consumed by greed, hatred, delusion, or free from these afflictions. The aim here is to cultivate wisdom and to let go of attachment and suffering.

Last, in the practice of mindfulness of phenomena, the Buddha teaches us to meditate on various aspects of reality such as the five hindrances, the five aggregates, the six sense fields, the seven awakening factors, and the four noble truths, guiding us toward deeper insight and liberation.

This vision of mindfulness extends far beyond our modern-day notion of merely being aware of the present moment without being judgmental. The Buddha taught mindfulness as keen observation of the body, feelings, mind, or phenomena, all carried out with a sense of detachment from desire, aversion, and other unwholesome states of mind.[19] The idea is to keep the mind constantly aware of when a negative or unskillful thought arises and restrain ourselves from acting on these thoughts. Once we master the art of nongrasping and maintaining equanimity toward all arising desires and defilements, our mind becomes purified, leading to liberation.

Mindfulness is a multifaceted practice that requires much commitment, effort, and patience. As such, to suggest that it's simply a practice of paying attention to the present moment without judgment is similar to saying driving is simply the act of paying attention to the road. Yes, that's one part of it, but there's so much more to it.

Take mindfulness of breathing alone, for instance. Mindfulness of breathing is just one part of the mindfulness of the body. The Buddha explains that focusing on our breath assists us in leaving behind our everyday worries or letting go of our normal thought patterns. It allows us to discover the beauty in the unlikeliest of places or to find positivity in difficult situations. It helps us remain calm, not swaying to the whims of good or bad events, and achieve deeper states of concentration and happiness, free from everyday distractions and negative emotions. As we become more skilled at mindful breathing, we'll be able to experience feelings without getting attached to them, understanding their transient nature and not being swept away by them.[20]

Imagine standing in a lush, green meadow with a calm river flowing nearby. This river carries away desires, aversions, and other unwholesome thoughts, leaving us in a state of utter tranquility. This idyllic scene is a metaphor for how the Buddha sees mindfulness, which is not about nonjudgmental observations of thoughts but a deep dedication to calming our inner storms to prevent them from bringing turmoil into our lives.

A verse in the EBTs often gets quoted to endorse the idea of "bare awareness" as a path to liberation: "In the seen will be merely the seen; in the heard will be merely the heard; in the thought will be merely the thought; in the known will be merely the known."[21]

At first glance, it might seem like we're encouraged to observe our sensory experiences with the same level of disinterest a teenager might display in a history class. But let's dig deeper.

The Buddha continues, stating that once we've mastered this detached perspective, we won't be "by that." When we're not "by that," we won't be "in that." And when we're not "in that," we find ourselves neither here in this world, nor there in the world beyond, or anywhere in between. It's as though we've stepped out of a relentless cosmic ping-pong game, marking the cessation of suffering. In essence, this is a profound discourse on ending our infatuation and identification with sensory experiences, ultimately paving the way to freedom from suffering.

This concentrated teaching gets more spotlight in another sutta, where the Buddha repeated the verses above before expanding: When we encounter a sight, sound, smell, taste, touch, or thought and get attached with desire, our mind descends into a whirlpool of greed and aversion. We become caught up in the cycle of wanting and not getting, a cycle that inevitably leads to suffering. However, through the application of mindfulness, we can ride the waves of these sensory experiences without falling into the trap of attachment and clinging. As we master this equilibrium, we don't accumulate suffering like an unstable Jenga tower; instead, suffering gradually fades away like a chalk drawing in the rain.[22]

To that end, it bears reemphasizing that mindfulness isn't a practice of nonjudgmental awareness. Rather, it's an active discipline that requires the absence of desire and aversion, a deep commitment to sensory restraint, a healthy degree of detachment, and a purification of all unwholesome thoughts, words, and actions. This nuance may sound as soft as a whisper, but it signifies a complete shift in understanding and practice.

The Buddha never advised us to refrain from judging our thoughts and feelings. While he cautioned against judging others, he championed the idea of us being our own sternest evaluators. When we notice greed, anger, and other harmful states of mind creeping within us, he taught us that we should identify these states for what they are and endeavor to transform them into wholesome states of mind such as generosity, patience, and loving-kindness. Just as a jeweler transforms a rough stone into a gleaming gem, the Buddha encouraged us to refine our thoughts, words, and actions. Our ultimate goal should be spiritual perfection, a state the Buddha himself embodied as the "Perfected One."

I understand why awareness without judgment has such a fan base—it's a cool breeze on a hot summer day, particularly for those who are dipping their toes into Buddhism. In a world that never stops judging, it's a comforting idea. This perspective fits hand in glove with our treasured American values of personal freedom and individuality, encouraging us to accept our family and friends and their experiences without judgment.

However, this lite version of mindfulness sparks some intriguing questions. What happens when someone with harmful thoughts is told to accept, embrace, or welcome those thoughts without judgment? Could this lead them to act on those thoughts? And a bigger question—by endorsing this diluted version of mindfulness, could we be losing sight of the heart of its transformative power?

Reflecting on these questions might lead us to recognize a recurring theme in secular Buddhism. In its effort to make Buddhist teachings more approachable, it seems to risk watering them down. This dilution becomes more conspicuous when we consider the ordained sangha, which has historically been a cornerstone in preserving the richness of Buddhist teachings.

The Role of the Sangha in America

In secular Buddhism, the role of ordained monks and nuns is generally overlooked. It's evident that secular Buddhism champions the cause of making Buddhism more accessible and relevant to those unable or unwilling to pursue the monastic path. This approach is not only pragmatic but also aligns with modern sensibilities. Secular Buddhism also advocates for a more egalitarian and democratic interpretation of Buddhism. In all these ways, secular Buddhism presents an appealing and contemporary face of Buddhism.

Yet it's important not to put all our eggs in one basket. The roles of traditional monastic communities shouldn't be diminished or disregarded. Their disciplined practices contribute to spiritual depth and the preservation of Buddhist teachings. As mentors, monastics inspire by exemplifying a life of simplicity and ethical integrity, standing in contrast to the materialistic tendencies of modern society. They are pivotal in cultivating ecological awareness and community engagement, offering more than just spiritual guidance but also educational resources and, on occasion, essential social services.

Imagine a monastery as a peaceful sanctuary nestled within a bustling city. Amid the rush-hour traffic and a relentless schedule, these serene places serve as a reminder that true joy and fulfillment stem not from external achievements or material possessions but are homegrown, blooming from inner wisdom, compassion, and peace. In this light, the ordained sangha can be seen as a countercultural movement, promoting a lifestyle focused on inner fulfillment rather than the pursuit of material wealth and status.

This Buddhist counternarrative isn't a theory; it has roots in the life of the Buddha himself. Born into royalty, he could have easily continued enjoying the luxuries of palace life. But the prince who could have had everything chose instead the bare essentials of robes, food, and shelter. This transition to a life focused on spiritual growth rather than material gain serves as a powerful testament to the transformative potential inherent in Buddhism.

In earlier chapters, I shared how my interest in Buddhism reignited after my study-abroad trip to Việt Nam in 2007.

Fifteen other University of Washington students and I explored the aftermath of the Vietnam-American war and the country's rebuilding efforts as well as engaged in reforestation projects and meetings with survivors of landmine incidents. The experience was like sipping a strong cup of black coffee, each bitter sip awakening deep, raw emotions within me.

In between this intensity, my oasis came in the form of tranquil temples and monasteries scattered throughout the country. The contrast was stark, almost surreal, like walking out of a heated debate and into a quiet library. A few steps onto the sacred grounds of these places and it felt as though I'd stepped through a magical portal into a realm of peace.

It struck me then that such oases are not mere afterthoughts in these societies; they are vital components of the cultural and spiritual ecosystem. And here lies a subtle but powerful difference: In many Asian societies, where Buddhism is woven into the fabric of life, supporting the monastic community is a social norm. In some countries, it's as second nature as saying "bless you" after a sneeze or leaving a tip at a restaurant. It's just something you do. Donations and government support make it possible for these spiritual places to offer free retreats, meals, and resources to the public, fostering a spirit of mutual support.

But here in America, it's a different story. Buddhist values aren't as widely recognized or appreciated, leading to a lack of adequate support. Moreover, many view Buddhism as a personal, sometimes solitary, journey, so they practice alone or in small groups. This trend, while not entirely negative, does stifle the emergence of large, interconnected communities that can serve as pillars of Buddhist wisdom and practice.

It was against this backdrop that the distinctions came into focus when I cofounded Cherry Blossom Sangha in 2016. We initially gathered in my apartment because no other options were available. As our group grew, we sought out a local practice center for more space. Understanding that these centers rely on contributions to sustain their operations, I was nevertheless taken aback by the forty-dollar fee for each gathering. This practice struck me as jarring, a stark departure from traditional Buddhist societies where supporting spiritual practice is seen as a noble obligation rather than a business transaction.

This dissonance between ideal and reality led me to an unconventional decision. Despite grappling with my own financial constraints—essentially from one paycheck to another—I took it upon myself to cover the rental costs for our sangha. I never considered asking members to chip in, viewing this not as charity on my part but as an opportunity for my own spiritual growth. Generosity, the Buddha teaches us, is not about relinquishing material possessions but about enriching our inner lives. It's an act that nurtures the mind through the joy of letting go, the freedom of giving, and the warmth of sharing with an open heart.[23] It's not about gaining brownie points or currying favor but strengthening our character and wisdom.[24] Reflecting on these acts of giving can foster a sense of spiritual contentment within us.[25] In the Buddha's words, "A good mood before giving, confidence while giving, feeling uplifted after giving: this is the perfect sacrifice."[26]

What these teachings illuminate so clearly is that while giving is traditionally viewed as a kindness toward others, in reality, it's the giver who stands to gain the most. It's a self-investment in our own spiritual and ethical development. Now, I recognize that in choosing to shoulder the costs myself, I may have unintentionally deprived others the same invaluable opportunity to cultivate this transformative generosity. Yet, what I grappled with was while some of my fellow sangha members may already be acquainted with the Buddha's teachings on generosity, I can't confidently say that a request for financial contributions would be universally accepted as a gateway to spiritual growth. For many, especially those who are less familiar with the nuances of dharma, the cost could instead present itself as an obstacle, a barrier that may deter them from deeper engagement with Buddhist practice. Given the rarity of encountering and embracing the dharma, the potential loss of those willing to walk this path weighed heavily on me; I could not justify the gamble.

This brings us to the crux of the matter: the task of nurturing a thriving Buddhist tradition within the American landscape, where Buddhism hasn't yet become an integral part of the societal fabric as it has in other parts of the world. A greater presence of monastics might significantly illuminate these teachings, encouraging a shift toward collective support within sanghas. These challenges, whether financial or cultural, amplify the need for a strong, well-established monastic community on US soil. The ordained sangha, fortified by centuries of wisdom, could serve as a guiding light, demystifying the dharma for newcomers and thereby making it more accessible. In such an environment, the practice of dana—the act of giving—could become normalized, laying the foundation for a robust Buddhist tradition where the financial, spatial, and cultural hindrances facing sanghas are simply remnants of a former time.

As the cultural tide in the United States gradually shifts, with more people seeking not just material prosperity but also spiritual depth and community well-being, the timing could not be more opportune for the emergence of a vibrant, homegrown American Buddhist monastic community. Such a community would not only support lay practitioners but also allow

American monastics to contribute meaningfully to American society at large.

However, for this vision to manifest, we must first acknowledge and address some of the unique challenges within the American Buddhist culture.

Meditation Isn't the Whole Story

The American ethos of independence and a general skepticism toward authority often lead people to prioritize meditation over moral teachings, but this imbalance can become a stumbling block on the path to genuine spiritual growth.

Consider Insight Meditation Society's annual three-month retreat, for instance. Participants meditate for up to fifteen hours a day. Spirit Rock's daily routine isn't much different, with seven forty-five-minute sitting sessions and six walking sessions. Yes, self-discovery through meditation is important, but an overemphasis on meditation at the expense of dharma study can lead to frustration and stunted spiritual development.

In *Why Buddhism Is True,* Robert Wright recounts such a struggle: "The first couple of days were excruciating . . . I could go a whole forty-five-minute meditation session without ever sustaining focus for ten consecutive breaths . . . I got mad at myself . . . madder and madder as the first couple of days wore on" (p. 19).

We Americans like to do things ourselves, to navigate life using our own internal compass. But the average American (you, me, hi, hello) can't simply meditate our way to enlightenment. The Buddha spent six years practicing and meditating in the forest before he achieved awakening. In our world, filled with nonstop social media, binge-worthy streaming services, and constant distractions, relying solely on meditation for a way out of suffering is like trying to swim upstream against a raging current.

We can't meditate without first understanding why we're unhappy or how to bring out that inner smile. The Buddha offered us a trove of teachings to explore, to ponder, and to apply in our lives. When we approach these teachings with open hearts and minds, they have the power to spark profound transformation and growth in us.

And the nice thing about the dharma? It's not exclusive. Even if we subscribe to a different faith, there's something in it for everyone. Insights that can help soothe our anxiety, fears, and other troubles.

In Việt Nam, when someone decides to pursue monasticism, they say they're going to *đi tu*. This phrase roughly translates to embarking on a journey of self-cultivation. And when a practitioner finds themselves grappling with challenges, they might say, "*Tôi tu yếu quá* ," which translates to "My cultivation is so weak."

In the EBTs, the Buddha proposed an array of cultivation methods and practices, yet he underscores the importance of the following: the four mindfulness meditations, the four right efforts, the four bases of mental power, the five faculties, the five powers, the seven awakening factors, and the eightfold path.[27] Authentic expressions of Buddhist modernism must be grounded in these fundamental teachings. We should provide practitioners with all of these tools, allowing them to discover which resonate and which do not.

Furthermore, Buddhist training zeros in on three key areas: higher ethics, higher mind, and higher wisdom.[28] Within this power trio, meditation, or the "higher mind," makes up just one-third, with mindfulness being merely one component of the eightfold path.

The Buddha outlined seven stepping stones—right view, thought, speech, action, livelihood, effort, and mindfulness—that guide us toward immersion, the grand finale of the eightfold path."[29]

Now, keep in mind that while these factors make up the eightfold path, they don't necessarily need to be practiced in a strict order. However, each one is essential to the journey, so it's not advisable to skip any steps. They're like different parts of a song—all working together to create a beautiful harmony.

Also, the term "right" in the eightfold path comes from the Pāli word *samma*, which can also be interpreted as "wise," "complete," "appropriate," or "in harmony." So the Buddha wasn't about dictating rights and wrongs but distinguishing between what's beneficial and what's not.

The main idea here is that following the seven stepping stones of the eightfold path prepares us for immersion into the four absorptions. This opens doors to feelings of joy, bliss, clarity, confidence, unity of mind, and equanimity. From this peaceful vantage point, we can explore our minds more deeply, leading to an extraordinary shift in our consciousness.

Newcomers to Buddhism who skip these essential factors and plunge directly into meditation may struggle to find the inner peace they yearn for. They are like gardeners attempting to grow plants in barren soil. Without cultivating the fertile ground of ethical conduct and wisdom development, the mind remains unsettled—like a leaf swirling in the wind—despite one's sincerest efforts at meditation.

Let's take a moment to visualize the Buddha's peaceful half-smile that we see in sculptures and paintings. His face a picture of serene calm, his smile radiating compassion and wisdom. It's an emblem of equanimity, a goal and reward for those committed to finding a haven within their own minds. To build this haven, we need more than meditation—we need a balanced integration of virtue, wisdom, and mental unification.

Realities and Aspirations of Modern Monasticism

The task of upholding and fortifying the ethical standards and wisdom of Buddhism largely falls on the ordained sangha. They do this by living their lives in accordance with the dharma, by teaching others about the dharma, and by providing a safe and supportive environment for those who are interested in learning about Buddhism.

The Buddha understood that for everyday folks, juggling the spiritual path with the whirlwind of daily life is like trying to text while riding a bike—not easy. In contrast, the life of a monastic, free from worldly ties, provides a more open and supportive atmosphere for spiritual practice. As he declares, "Living in a house is cramped, but the life of one gone forth is wide open. It's not easy for someone living at home to lead the spiritual life utterly full and pure, like a polished shell."[30] He also reminds us that our success in spiritual practice is tied to our commitment. If we practice partially, we succeed partially; if we practice fully, we succeed fully.[31]

The Buddha outlines the kind of lifestyle that sets a sage—a term he used for the ideal monastic—apart from the average person. A sage prefers hanging out in quiet spots over crowded places, seeks wisdom, embodies kindness, and practices mindfulness. They avoid wickedness and know the difference between right and wrong. They have no interest in intimate relationships and procreation. They've navigated the tumultuous seas of life, reached their spiritual goals, and now stand unattached and free. This sage, disciplined and compassionate, seeks to protect all living beings, while the average individual may harm creatures. Therefore, a person engrossed in worldly concerns can't match the inner peace of a sage, who finds tranquility through meditation in the forest.[32]

Granted, many monastics today grapple with meeting this lofty ideal. But just because a few may have let us down, it would be unwise to toss out the whole idea of monasticism. After all, renunciation is the heartbeat of Buddhism, with monasticism the lifeblood pumping through its veins.

Life as a monastic, if we dive into it with an open heart, can be deeply fulfilling. We learn to replace our narrow, exclusive kinds of love for something more expansive, boundless, and inclusive. In doing so, we get to taste happiness that's independent of external factors—a spiritual bliss that the Buddha considered the pinnacle of joy.[33] When we go all in on this spiritual journey, we forge deeper connections with everything around us. This can cause our ego to shrink down to the size of a pea, opening up vast opportunities for personal growth and transformation.

In this light, it becomes clear that to unlock the full promise of Buddhism in American culture, a more intentional and focused effort is needed. Without the anchor of a robust monastic community offering guidance and inspiration, we risk reducing Buddhism to another facet of America's medley of lifestyle options rather than allowing it to flourish as the profound spiritual path it was intended to be.

As a dynamic religion, Buddhism has managed to thrive wherever it has been planted. It's like a tree that grows strong, no matter the soil or weather. In the United States, our challenge lies in recognizing the rich value of dharma and monasticism, integrating them with our cultural context to harmonize with American sensibilities.

The Buddha himself championed this flexibility. He says the sangha could abolish some minor rules after he is gone.[34] He advocates for the dharma to be learned in one's own language.[35] He shares stories about instances when he blends in with various groups; his "appearance and voice became just like theirs" as he sits with them, converses, and engages in discussion.[36] He recognizes that different people learn in different ways, and he is able to adapt his teaching style to meet the needs of each audience. He also instructs his followers to ensure that the propagation of dharma isn't confined to a single path but winds its way through individual journeys, enriching the world one person at a time.[37]

In the diverse landscape of America, some might doubt Buddhism's ability to make a significant impact, citing its relatively recent arrival in our cultural discourse. But I see things differently. The intersection between Buddhism and America in this moment presents an exceptional opportunity. The cultural, racial, linguistic, and experiential diversity that America offers paves the way for an American monastic community that mirrors our shared values—a community that champions mutual respect, harmony, and compassion, strengthened by the multitude of viewpoints and voices. A community where individuals from all walks of life converge to explore and practice the dharma. A community that serves as a beacon of hope and inspiration in a world often marred by violence, division, and conflict.

In America, we pride ourselves on pushing boundaries, on challenging the status quo. It's in this spirit that we can reconceptualize Buddhism. Our goal isn't to create a "new" Buddhism—the essence of the dharma already echoes our values of equality, liberty, and opportunity. What we're talking about here is an evolution—a refinement in our approach to practicing Buddhism that liberates us from the confines of patriarchy, misogyny, and other harmful practices.

The responsibility rests on our shoulders to ensure that Buddhism in America does not lose its way in the maze of social dysfunction and culture wars. Let us stand united in building an American Buddhism—one infused with purpose, guided by compassion, and deeply rooted in our shared vision for the future of Buddhism and the world.

8

Gun Rights

What Would the Buddha Say?

In a time when society often seems more divided than united, one may wonder: Could the philosophies of Buddhism offer a bridge over the chasms that define our days? This chapter aims to examine Buddhism's lens on nonviolence and its potential resonance with contemporary America—a nation grappling with senseless acts of violence and deeply polarized public opinion. It should be stated at the outset that this exploration is not designed to challenge the Second Amendment or to provoke partisan discord. Instead, it explores how Buddhist teachings, emphasizing compassion, moral responsibility, and the interconnectedness of all beings, might offer alternative responses to contemporary societal challenges.

At the cornerstone of Buddhism is an unwavering commitment to harmlessness. The Buddha's directive is unequivocal: "Do not kill any creature, nor have them killed, nor grant permission for others to kill. Lay aside violence towards all creatures, frail or firm, that there are in the world."[1] His teachings go beyond mere injunctions; they articulate a framework of moral responsibility and emotional intelligence that all beings—be it a tiny bug or an individual marred by misdeeds—deserve kindness and consideration.[2]

Further fortifying this ethos, the Buddha advises against engaging in certain livelihoods—trading in weapons, living beings, meat, intoxicants, and poisons—that perpetuate harm and suffering.[3] Occupations that inflict violence or harm on others were strongly discouraged, ranging from those of a slaughterer and an executioner to even more socially accepted roles like that of a hunter.[4]

A common thread in Buddhist morality is the understanding that all beings desire happiness and freedom from pain. The Buddha urges us to reflect on our own desire for happiness and extend that same desire to others: "I want to live, be happy, and not be in pain. If someone hurts me, I wouldn't like it. Everyone else probably feels the same way. If I hurt someone else, they wouldn't like it either. And if someone stole from me, lied to me, broke my friendships, yelled at me, or annoyed me, I wouldn't like it. What I don't like, others probably don't like too. Knowing that, how can I do any of those things to someone else?"[5]

Building on this foundational principle, the Buddha also provides a poetic expression of the moral imperative to recognize the universality of life's joys and sorrows:

All tremble at the rod,
all fear death.
Treating others like oneself,
neither kill nor incite to kill.

All tremble at the rod,
all love life.
Treating others like oneself,
neither kill nor incite to kill.[6]

Once, King Pasenadi of Kosala asked his queen, Mallikā, if there was anyone she loved more than herself. Her response echoed the truth universally felt: "No, great king, there isn't. Is there anyone more dear to you than yourself?" The king's answer mirrored his queen's sentiment—no one held a place in his heart dearer than himself.

Reflecting on this exchange, the Buddha said, "Having explored every quarter with the mind, likewise for others, each holds themselves dear; so one who loves themselves would harm no other."[7]

The Buddha's teachings go deeper. He posits that individuals who harm themselves or others are, in essence, betraying their self-love. The Buddha advises, "If you're doing bad things by way of body, speech, and mind, you don't love yourself because you're treating yourself like an enemy. But if you truly love yourself, you'd do good things by way of body, speech, and mind and make an effort to end all defilements."[8]

This guidance on self-love is a powerful reminder that love and respect begin within. We ought to embrace ourselves with the same kindness and compassion that we would show others, aiming to lead lives that enrich both our own existence and that of others.

The Buddha believes the root of violence and conflict in our world comes from five sensory delights: mesmerizing sights, enchanting sounds, bewitching fragrances, delicious tastes, and enticing touches. These pleasures, like a mighty storm, can incite kings to wars and turn families against their own. Even the sacred bond between a mother and child can be broken by this storm of desire. In the face of overpowering yearning, people resort to violence, leaving behind a trail of blood and heartache.[9]

The Buddha teaches that when we are attached to these pleasures, we are constantly seeking them out and are never satisfied. But when we let go of our attachment and selfishness, we are free to experience the world in all its fullness, without the need for constant stimulation. We are free to be happy simply because we are alive.

In the *Taking Up Arms Sutta*, the Buddha warns about the dangers of wielding weapons, underscoring that it leads to a cycle of fear and violence. He speaks of the emotional and mental "darts" that pierce the human heart, inciting people to run around in a state of confusion, conflict, and despair. Removing these darts—which are symbolic of attachments and desires—brings about a state of inner stillness that prevents destructive behaviors. He calls for ethical conduct, truthfulness, and equanimity as pathways out of the moral mire we might find ourselves in.[10]

In the context of the current debate on gun rights and gun violence, this teaching urges us to question the deep-rooted fears and attachments that contribute to a culture of violence. Peace isn't merely the absence of conflict but requires an inner transformation—achieved by removing the "darts" of ignorance, attachment, fear, and other unwholesome states of mind. Equanimity and safety lie in mastery over our minds and emotions, not in our capacity to wield weapons.

In the same vein, when faced with violence and conflict, the Buddha advises us to maintain our hearts full of love and compassion. In his own words, "Our minds will remain unaffected. We will blurt out no bad words. We will remain full of compassion, with a heart of love and no secret hate. We will meditate spreading a heart of love to that person. And with them as a basis, we will meditate spreading a heart full of love to everyone in the world—abundant, expansive, limitless, free of enmity and ill will."[11]

On the flip side, the Buddha denounces those who seek to slay their enemies, labeling such a mindset "low, degraded, and misdirected." He argues that not only are such actions harmful and unskillful, but those who believe they will receive heavenly rewards for violent deeds are operating under a misguided view.[12]

The Complex Web of Karma and Social Justice

The concept of karma—the law of cause and effect—asserts that our actions are linked to their consequences. What we do shapes our lives and ripples out to touch others. As such, we're duty-bound to act in ways that nurture happiness and well-being for all. Plant seeds of joy, and we'll harvest happiness. Sow seeds of corruption or violence, and we'll reap a bitter harvest of suffering.[13] It's that simple.

Yet while karma shapes our present reality, the Buddha recognizes that a multitude of factors, including social conditions, environmental factors, and genetics, can influence our current state. In a conversation with a man named Moḷiyasīvaka, he clarify that not all life experiences result from past karma. Some arise from physical causes, changes in the weather, neglect of self-care, or overexertion.[14] He encourages us to recognize this complex web of causes and conditions that shape our lives, urging us not to reduce everything to past actions but to acknowledge the complexity of life's causality.

When addressing societal conflicts, the Buddha compares violence and retaliation with fanning a fire in an attempt to extinguish it—in other words, they don't work. An exercise in futility. He stresses the importance of addressing the underlying causes of these issues, much like a doctor would treat the cause of an illness, not just the symptoms.

To illustrate this point, he once told a story about King Mahāvijita, whose kingdom was riddled with crime and poverty. Bandits caused mayhem, sowing terror in the hearts of villagers and city dwellers alike. The king considered pacifying this chaos through harsh measures such as execution, imprisonment, or banishment. But the Buddha advised that these retaliatory actions would only provide temporary relief. Instead, he proposed a deeper solution—support farmers and cattle herders, fund trades, and ensure that workers receive fair food and wages. He encouraged the king to transform the country into a just and supportive sanctuary so that people could live happily and securely without fear.[15]

This age-old wisdom holds relevance for modern America as we struggle with persistent issues like crime and recidivism. Our justice system seems fixated on punitive measures as deterrents, yet it fails at reducing crime rates or preventing released individuals from sliding back into their old patterns.

Perhaps, taking inspiration from the Buddha's advice to King Mahāvijita, we should reconsider our approach. Maybe a more compassionate, holistic strategy serves us better. Addressing the root causes of crime by investing in education, affordable housing, mental health services, drug rehab programs, and employment services—these could equip individuals to build resilience, learn new skills, and find a supportive community that aids in making better life choices.

It's worth noting that the Buddha was not naive about the world's harsh realities. He was well aware that violence and conflict are inevitable aspects of our human existence and that nations must be ready to safeguard their citizens in times of turmoil.[16] However, for those of us on a spiritual journey, recognizing the interconnectedness in all beings compels us to confront and transform our deepest internal adversaries—intolerance, prejudice, discrimination—through self-awareness, open dialogue, and a willingness to change. In this light, there is no justification for bearing arms.[17] Our life's mission is to foster peace, love, and understanding, both within ourselves and toward others.[18] When faced with another's suffering, our instinct isn't to stoke the flames of conflict but rather to douse them with the cooling balm of compassion.

The Buddha's timeless wisdom offers a potent reminder: "Hatred is never settled by hate, but only by love. This is the eternal law."[19] This enduring truth, as relevant today as it was during his time, challenges us to respond to hatred *not* with more of the same but with love. Love is the universal principle. It is the path to peace and the keystone of a life lived in harmony with oneself and the world around us.

9

Gay Marriage

What Would the Buddha Say?

The Buddha's silence on the subject of homosexuality in the EBTs has left many of us pondering about his stance on gay marriage. Some, yearning for clarity, have relied on sources outside of the EBTs, such as later traditions or various teachers. But let's keep in mind that the Buddha's teachings offer a comprehensive ethical framework, illuminating his perspectives on sexuality and relationships.

The five precepts provide the moral bedrock for lay Buddhists, the fundamental guiding principles. The Buddha spells it out clearly: "A noble disciple refrains from taking life, stealing, engaging in sexual misconduct, lying, or indulging in alcoholic drinks that cause negligence."[1]

So how does the Buddha define "sexual misconduct"? In several discourses, he laid out the concept as follows: "Having sexual relations with someone protected by their parents, siblings, relatives, or clan. Or someone promised to another, married, or prohibited by law. Such bodily behavior causes unskillful qualities to grow while skillful qualities decline."[2]

One should bear in mind that the above is all the Buddha said about sexual misconduct in the EBTs. He didn't address homosexuality when discussing sexual misconduct. His teachings steered monastics away from any sexual activity and advised followers to avoid harmful acts like adultery and nonconsensual or unlawful sex. And that, essentially, is the extent of it.

Fast-forward a few centuries, and we find texts with more explicit views. The fourth- or fifth-century Indian Buddhist scholar Vasubandhu's *Treasury of Metaphysics with Self-Commentary* set limitations on nonvaginal sex. The authors of the *Great Nirvāṇa Sūtra* labeled individuals who didn't identify as male or female as "evil-rooted." Jump to the twentieth century, and Chinese Chán master Hsuan Hua stated in his book, *Avoid Defying Natural Creation*, that homosexuality contradicts procreation and thus constitutes sexual misconduct. In 1997, the Dalai Lama affirmed full human rights for everyone, no matter their sexual orientation. But then he added a proviso, suggesting that from a Buddhist view, same-sex relations could be considered sexual misconduct.

Yeshe Rabgye, a British monk who practices within the Tibetan Buddhism Kagyu tradition, offers additional insight into this diverse spectrum of views. He proposes that the Dalai Lama's outlook might be rooted in the teachings of Je Tsongkhapa, an influential Tibetan monk from the fifteenth century. Tsongkhapa's guidelines on sexual conduct, reflective of broader Tibetan and Indian Buddhist traditions, were intricate. He disapproved of male-to-male sex but condoned female-to-female. Solo acts, oral and anal sex, and sexual activities during the day were no-gos. But he greenlighted men climaxing five times during the nighttime and visiting sex workers. He even created a checklist of okay and not-okay body parts, timings, and locations.

This leads us to confront a recurring theme in Buddhism's history: the rules and texts, traditionally penned by men, often seem to conveniently favor men. And it's not just any men but heterosexual men, who not only form the societal majority but also hold the reins of power, allowing them to assert dominance and shape the religion to align with their interests and perspectives.

In the face of these varying viewpoints, we can turn to the Buddha's own teachings for guidance. As a compassionate teacher whose primary concern was the alleviation of suffering, the Buddha wasn't one to provide a detailed manual for our bedroom activities. Instead, he encouraged us to shun actions that cause harm to ourselves and others. His moral instructions for laypeople can be boiled down to this: "Refrain from taking life, stealing, and sexual misconduct. Refrain from speech that's false, divisive, harsh, or nonsensical. Contentment, kind-heartedness, and wise view: these things are skillful."[3]

As noted earlier, the Buddha required celibacy among monastics, discouraging any kind of intimacy or sexual relations whatsoever. This prohibition is universal, applying equally to all monastics regardless of gender or orientation. Violating the vow of celibacy results in immediate expulsion from the sangha, with no exceptions.

While the Buddha's instructions were clear, the waters get murkier when we delve into how these precepts have evolved over time. Unraveling the evolution of monastic discipline is like attempting a three-dimensional jigsaw puzzle—it's a complex and multilayered endeavor. However, one irrefutable fact remains: a good chunk of the Vinaya text, the rulebook for monastics, was added later. Some scholars believe the original rules only prohibited heterosexual relations for monastics, with additional categories such as *ubhatovyañjanaka* (hermaphrodite) and *paermap* (eunuch) introduced over time. These additions demonstrate the Vinaya's flexibility, reflecting societal norms more than the Buddha's original teachings.

Presently, several Buddhist schools and traditions outright refuse to ordain individuals who don't conform to the traditional gender binary. Prominent commentators such as Buddhaghosa and Vasubandhu depict these individuals as spiritually deficient or sexually deviant. These perspectives, which starkly contrast with the principles of universal compassion and respect for all beings intrinsic to Buddhism, indicate a dismissive stance toward nontraditional sexual and gender identities.

These sentiments align with past global attitudes, where homosexuality was universally criminalized. Yet, the world is slowly but surely moving toward a more empathetic and inclusive understanding of human sexuality. Laws that once criminalized homosexuality are increasingly being archived in the dusty shelves of history. It seems inevitable that love, compassion, and understanding—these powerful forces for good—will ultimately prevail over ignorance, prejudice, and discrimination. It is my firm belief that future generations will look back at our age of banned same-sex marriage with a combination of disbelief, shame, and regret.

In the EBTs, the Buddha advocates against looking down on anyone because of their livelihood, intelligence, or commitments.[4] He emphasizes that all labels we attach to people are social constructs, not reflections of their intrinsic worth. Our sense of identity sprouts from a web of perceptions, rooted in our underlying tendencies such as repulsions, doubts, and conceit.[5]

Understanding this, the Buddha identifies attachment to these constructs as a lower fetter that needs to be eradicated.[6] To achieve this, we must cultivate a sense of "not-self" in all things,[7] stepping beyond labels and tuning into the boundless potential of our true nature.[8]

The Genderless Ideal

Picture a time before human existence. The world was home to luminous ethereal beings, neither male nor female. As these radiant beings started consuming solid food and became more physical, their light dimmed. They noticed differences among themselves, evolving into diverse appearances. Some were strikingly beautiful, others not as much. Women started to look like women and men like men. As sensual desires ramped up, their bodies ignited with passion, and they, well—they got busy.[9]

While scholars consider this account in the EBTs a cosmogonical myth, it reinforces a recurring theme in the early texts—that our individual and societal suffering springs from an unquenchable thirst for sensual pleasures. As such, the ideal type of being is characterized by identical, sexless, asensual, and androgynous humans. Gender distinctions are depicted as the result of moral decline in the form of greed and lust, while the superior human form is neither male nor female but genderless.

This theme echoes again when the Buddha explains how men and women entangle themselves with each other due to their attachment to gender identity and the pleasure that comes with interacting with the opposite gender. The key to untying this knot is to let go of the attachment to gender identity and the pleasure it brings. By doing so, we bridge the gender divide and inch closer to liberation.[10]

We can see this quest to transcend fixed views of gender manifests in monastic practices, like wearing plain robes or shaving one's hair. It's about snipping away attachments to appearances. The less we identify with our physical selves, the closer we come to self-transcendence.

Fostering a Manifold Sangha in Modern Times

The Buddha's sangha was an embodiment of inclusivity, welcoming all beings irrespective of birth or social standing. Every member was acknowledged equally, and the door was open to individuals from all walks of life, including infamous criminals like Aṅgulimāla and courtesans like Aḍḍhakāsī. In light of this, it's hard to imagine the Buddha turning away someone yearning to join his ministry based on their sexual orientation or identity. After all, homosexuality is when individuals are attracted to others of the same sex, and heterosexuality is when the attraction is toward individuals of a different sex. The yearning to love and be loved by another—how can this cause harm? It doesn't. Unlike criminal behavior or sex work, which can have complex and often negative impacts, love in any form is inherently harmless and should not be conflated with the traditional criteria for monastic ordination.

When the day fades into night, all monastics, regardless of their biological makeup or social identities, are expected to uphold celibacy. The essence of renunciation lies in saying goodbye to sensual desires. One's gender orientation and biological makeup have no bearing on one's capacity for ethical and spiritual growth.

One of the Buddha's teachings underscores the point that awakening is a universal potential. Anyone can attain enlightenment. It goes something like this: "Think of a cattle. No matter its color, if it's tamed and strong, it can bear the load. Its color doesn't matter; it's all about its capabilities. Similarly, with humans, it doesn't matter where they're born or what they look like. A tamed individual of good manners, grounded in Dharma, virtuous, and truthful, can achieve spiritual perfection."[11]

This teaching is something to take to heart as we strive for inclusivity and equality within the Buddhist community. The sangha, often promoted as fourfold, should really be manifold, embracing individuals of all identities. If we truly follow the Buddha's teachings, then the question of whether to accept nonconforming gender ordination or same-sex marriage should reflect our commitment to inclusivity.

The Buddha once drew a compelling analogy to underscore the principle of equality among his disciples. Just as rivers lose their unique names when they merge into the ocean, our individual identities, including all social distinctions, dissolve when we join the sangha. We simply become Sakyan ascetics, or members of the Buddha's community, united in the shared pursuit of freedom.[12]

When we join the sangha, we're taking a step toward this freedom. Acknowledging our varied identities, we link arms with a larger community of beings. We become a part of an interconnected web of life—a connection that binds us to one another and the natural world. This is the ultimate embodiment of equanimous unity.

10

Walking the Middle Path between Privilege and Prejudice

For over two thousand years, the Buddha's teachings have traveled across mountains and oceans, finding a home in the hearts of people from all walks of life. Yet if we take a moment to look at the American Buddhist community today, we might notice that it's not as diverse as one might hope. The prominence of white lay teachers and authors within American Buddhism raises important questions about representation. While not inherently problematic, this skew suggests a potential mismatch between the diversity of Buddhism's followers and the voices most often heard in its Western iteration.

It's an observation that can't be ignored and prompts us to ask: Is the true breadth of the Buddha's teachings being fully represented in the American context? Understanding the complex relationship among privilege, social responsibility, and cultural influences is crucial, but it's not straightforward. It's a tangle of factors that deserves careful and sensitive examination if we want to see genuine growth and inclusivity in US Buddhism.

From my perspective, as a woman of both ethnic and religious minority backgrounds, I've noticed a tableau of missed opportunities and cultural stagnation. While there are instances of cultural misunderstandings and privilege affecting the spread of the dharma, there's also evidence of transformative change when wisdom and compassion are wielded with thoughtful intent.

For white Americans, particularly those with social influence, there's a unique and important opportunity here. The Buddha's teachings offer more than individual growth; they provide a framework for societal betterment. Embracing these teachings with authenticity has the potential to breathe new life into American Buddhism and might contribute to addressing broader social and systemic inequities.

According to the 2020 US Census, white Americans make up 57.8 percent of the population, yet their influence is disproportionately vast in politics, economy, and culture. A 2019 Federal Reserve study illustrates this: the median white household boasts $180,000 in wealth compared with $24,000 for Black households and $36,000 for Latine ones.

Step into the corporate world, and the imbalance persists. A 2020 Fortune report shows that 90 percent of Fortune 500 CEOs are white. Fast-forward to 2023, and Congress largely mirrors this disparity, with white members making up 77 percent of its body. As for the 2023 Forbes Real-time Billionaires List, it's pretty much the same story. White American men continue to hold a significant majority of the world's wealth, with only a few exceptions to break the mold.

So what does all this mean for the average white American? For many, walking down the street without feeling judged might seem as natural as breathing. Expecting fair treatment by law enforcement? That's usually in the bag. Seeing role models who look like them in movies, news, or books? In places in Seattle, that's as common as rain—and trust me, it rains a lot here. But these so-called everyday experiences aren't everyday for everyone. For many people of color, these freedoms, these certainties of life, are more like rare gems than commonplace stones.

Given this landscape of racial and economic disparities, where does Buddhism fit in? Can it offer any answers to these deep-seated concerns that are so much a part of our society?

Dismantling Inequality

White Buddhists find themselves at a unique intersection where the path of privilege meets the transformative teachings of Buddhism—teachings that emphasize interconnectedness, the concept of not-self, and universal compassion. These aren't just lofty concepts; they're actionable principles with implications that ripple far and wide. They carry the potential not only to reshape Buddhist communities into vibrant hubs of inclusivity but also to radiate this change outward, influencing American society and the world at large. These principles can amplify teachings that catalyze social harmony and justice, empower voices that have been marginalized by systemic imbalances, and confront critical societal issues like racism and sexism both within and beyond spiritual circles.

The Buddha was unwavering in his stance that the ethical dimensions of wealth are determined not by its mere possession but by how we acquire it and how we use it. This aligns closely with his teachings on "wise livelihood," which advocates for going about our business in a decent, ethical way; earning our keep without harming others; and spreading the love and wealth around when we can.[1]

As discussed in chapter 7, the Buddha's teachings on giving illuminate how a generous act is far more than a mere transaction. It's a spiritual and ethical practice that enriches our hearts and minds, freeing us from the clutch of greed and fostering a spirit of communal sharing. He encourages us to give without the shadow of anticipation for something in return hanging over our actions.[2] He emphasizes, "If sentient beings only knew, as I do, the fruit of giving and sharing, they would not eat without first giving, and the stain of stinginess would not occupy their minds. They would not eat without sharing even their last mouthful, their last morsel, so long as there was someone to receive it."[3]

Now let's flip that and look at the towering wealth that America boasts. As of 2021, the United States has been home to over 140,000 millionaires, each worth more than $50 million. In terms of collective wealth, the United States outshines every other country with a staggering $106 trillion, more than the combined wealth of the next four wealthiest nations—China, Japan, Germany, and the United Kingdom.

And yet the US Census Bureau reveals that 11.5 percent of Americans were living in poverty in 2022. Marginalized communities—especially in the southern and western United States—are grappling with layers of economic disadvantages. These inequities multiply for those carrying additional burdens of marginalization, be it Black or brown races, gender, sexual orientation, disability, criminal history, or religious beliefs.

To understand the moral implications of wealth and sharing, we can turn to *A Rainless Cloud Sutta*. Here, the Buddha presents a timeless metaphor of three kinds of people and their approach to wealth. The first type is like a rainless cloud—they amass wealth but give nothing away. The second type is a notch better—they share their wealth selectively, like a cloud raining only on a particular area. The most commendable person is like a cloud that showers the whole earth—they share their wealth with anyone in need.[4]

Imagine how much the world would change if everyone with a brimming treasure chest took this teaching to heart. The impact would be immediate and transformative. The erasure of hunger and poverty wouldn't be a dream but an attainable reality.

But the Buddha doesn't stop at sharing wealth; he goes deeper. He offers a potent antidote: replace the three mental "poisons" of ignorance, greed, and hatred with wisdom, generosity, and compassion. This goes beyond cultivating love[5] and renouncing hatred;[6] we need to view the entire world with equanimity—a state of mind that's clear, calm, and free from bias and ill will.[7]

Equanimity in Buddhism isn't just about maintaining calm and composure but adopting an even-handed attitude toward everything in the world, viewed through the lens of unity.[8] To reach this equilibrium, the Buddha teaches that we must go beyond tolerating diversity and immerse ourselves in understanding everyone and everything as part of an interconnected, global family.[9]

The Buddha speaks of two kinds of equanimity. The first type, grounded in diversity, is limited by its attachment to worldly distinctions and differences and does not address the root causes of our discomfort. It's like trying to find peace while clinging to the very things that divide us. The second type, grounded in unity, transcends such barriers. This type understands the common thread interwoven among all things. It bids farewell to the tiny details that divide us and welcomes the commonalities that unite us. Choosing this path of unity liberates us from inner turmoil and fosters harmony with the world. In this expansive state, our sense of self dissolves, becoming not a separate entity but an integral part of the global consciousness.

Beyond the Labels Society Assigns

Residing in Seattle as a Vietnamese American, I recognize the privileges I've been afforded. I can live in any neighborhood and feel welcomed. I've been offered employment for nearly every job I interviewed for, and while my education and experiences play a significant role, I am mindful that my identity as a female minority may also make me the diverse candidate organizations actively seek to fulfill their inclusive hiring goals. When I disclose my Vietnamese heritage, people often soften their gazes and light up with curiosity, sympathy, or a blend of both. They may share their fondness for Vietnamese food or experiences from their travels.

Now, as much as I value these encounters, they also trigger a yearning within me to illuminate the fact that my Vietnamese background is just one aspect of my multifaceted identity. Being born in Việt Nam and raised in the United States was not a choice but a result of circumstance. I hold various roles—a daughter, a sister, an aunt, a former dance and drill team captain, a city governance professional, and a sports enthusiast who loves basketball, badminton, and volleyball. I find joy in Pinterest-ing recipes, learning the art of cooking, collecting lipsticks of all colors, and spending time with my parents' dogs, Goku and Plato. My identity is further colored by the fluidity of my attractions, where my heterosexuality occasionally blurs as I find myself drawn to the charm of tomboyish women.

My identity is dynamic, changing with each new experience and lesson learned. Life's journey is a living story, reflecting not just of who we are, but also the potential within all of us to evolve when we embrace the full spectrum of our beings.

Just as the Buddha taught that our identities are as fluid as ocean waves, constantly in motion, holding tight to a single perception of self is like trying to clutch water in our hands—it's futile and leads to suffering. True wisdom lies in recognizing the common threads that bind us all—the shared human experience and the universal yearning for happiness, health, love, and respect.

This perspective doesn't just underscore our shared humanity but also challenges the boxes society insists on placing us in. Imagine the liberation in tearing off these labels like taking off a heavy backpack we've been carrying around for years. Life feels lighter, freer, and more open—freeing us to express our unique gifts, chase our dreams, and live our lives on our own terms.

If we all truly grasped the Buddha's wisdom about the fluidity of identity and the interconnectedness of all beings, then the unsettling days of the COVID-19 pandemic wouldn't have shaken my sense of belonging in America. When face masks became a public mandate, I was met with unfamiliar, probing stares. I could see curiosity and an undercurrent of resentment in the eyes of strangers. A longing slowly but surely emerged in me to ease their uncertainty, to affirm my Vietnamese heritage, and to express that Wuhan was as much a mystery to me as to them. Eventually, I found a gentle way to communicate this in the virtual world: by adding Vietnamese tone marks to my name on Zoom and other platforms. As the pandemic cast its shadow on all our lives, I wanted to shield myself from the unnecessary hostility brewing in this time of great uncertainty.

If this was my reality, can you imagine the ordeal Chinese Americans had to bear and continue to face? The pandemic era was a mirror held up to my face, revealing the privilege I had been unknowingly enjoying. With the utmost respect, I believe I felt a sliver of what it might be like to be Black, Native American, or Latine in America. The concept of "otherness" became a lived reality, not an abstract idea. I was suddenly self-conscious, stepping cautiously into a world where vulnerability was the norm for many.

Still, comparatively speaking, Asians often find themselves in a more favorable position relative to other marginalized groups. So despite the pandemic's challenges, I still count myself fortunate. I continue to see my cup as half full, teeming with possibilities.

This takes me to the dicey topic of Asian privilege, exemplified by recent legal battles against affirmative action, like the June 2023 Supreme Court ruling in *Students for Fair Admissions v. Harvard*. In this landmark case, the Court ruled 6–2 that Harvard's affirmative action program violated the Equal Protection Clause of the Fourteenth Amendment. The suit, brought forth by a nonprofit organization advocating for race-neutral admissions, accused Harvard of lowering admission scores for Asian American applicants in favor of other racial groups.

This lawsuit exposes the fine line between advocating for our community and undermining others who have endured more significant systemic obstacles. It also reveals an uncomfortable truth: Asian Americans can be quick to rally for their own causes but equally quick to align with majority viewpoints when it serves them. In other words, we demand justice when feeling shortchanged but stay conspicuously silent when the scale tips in our favor at the expense of other marginalized communities. This selective engagement harms broader social justice initiatives and betrays the very communities whose struggles paved the way for the rights we now enjoy. Genuine commitment to justice is about persisting in advocacy, especially for those most underserved, regardless of the complexities or challenges that may arise.

The Buddha's teachings stand firmly against all forms of prejudice or inequality. They echo with themes of inclusivity, equality, and nondiscrimination, evidenced in the thousands—literally thousands—of discourses in the EBTs.

Consider, for instance, the Buddha's warning about three toxic ways of seeing ourselves in relation to others—as superior, inferior, or even as equals if it stems from a place of rivalry. These attitudes are pitfalls that can steer us down the wrong path, resulting in behaviors such as favoritism and hostility.[10]

On the other hand, imagine a world without the ego's loudspeaker, where thoughts of *I* and *mine* don't run the show. In that realm, we find a peace that doesn't play favorites or pick sides. A sense of peace in harmony with the world around us, free from the chains of judgments, self-importance, and identity.[11]

The Buddha speaks of four superpowers we should aspire to: wisdom, energy, blamelessness, and inclusiveness.[12] Among these, inclusiveness manifests through acts of giving, speaking kindly, offering care, and practicing equality.[13]

He cautions against the dangers of intolerance, judgment, or discrimination, noting that such behavior ultimately backfires, hurting us instead.[14]

In sterner tones, the Buddha describes those who abandon moral principles, are influenced by bias and hatred, and give in to unchecked cravings as "an assembly of the dregs."[15] In plain terms, these are individuals who are morally corrupt and who will only hold us back. To rise above this, we need to shake off those ego-driven attributes like arrogance, feelings of inferiority or superiority, overconfidence, and stubbornness.[16]

The Buddha also advocates against clinging to rigid beliefs and attitudes, describing them as a breeding ground for conflict. He elucidates:

> If you think that "I'm equal,
> special, or worse," you'll get into arguments.
> Unwavering in the face of the three discriminations,
> you'll have no thought "I'm equal or special".
> There are no ties for one detached from ideas;
> there are no delusions for one freed by wisdom.
> But those who have adopted ideas and views
> wander the world causing conflict.[17]

The above teaching is like music to my ears—timeless wisdom about letting go of our fixed views that rings with significance in the contemporary world.

Today, we witness the struggle with this concept on a nearly daily basis, where the rigidity of extremist groups—be they political, religious, or ideological—radiates waves of distress and suffering due to their inflexibility and unwillingness to entertain different viewpoints.

A striking example of this is the stark political polarization that has gripped America in recent years. We're seeing friendships end, families split, and a Congress so stuck that it can barely pass any laws. It's tearing apart the sense of community that holds a nation together. Like the Buddha warns, clinging to rigid beliefs only serves to cause conflict and suffering. He emphasizes releasing biases and refraining from deeming our viewpoint as the "absolute truth." He promotes a broad, impartial outlook as a cornerstone for nurturing peace and mutual understanding.[18]

He also spoke against the pitfalls of puffing up our egos[19] and putting people down.[20] He teaches that if we're genuinely wise, we'd act with restraint and never resort to insult.[21] We'd know the difference between right and wrong and recoil from wicked deeds.[22] On the flip side, if we're consumed by possessions, honor, and popularity, we'd eventually suffer lasting harm.[23]

So what does this mean for race and diversity in American Buddhism? If white practitioners truly take these teachings to heart, we could expect to see a more diverse landscape in our sanghas and a surge in Black, Indigenous, and people of color voices in Buddhist literature.

Moreover, a Buddhism steeped in humility wouldn't be commodified or whitewashed for mainstream tastes. It would value the wisdom each unique perspective brings rather than diluting its teachings to conform to commercial norms.

Finally, if white Buddhists were truly committed to these teachings, they'd take a strong stand against intolerance, bigotry, and discrimination. This wouldn't just be doing the right thing; it would affirm that such conduct is fundamentally incompatible with the essence of Buddhism.

Finding Common Ground while Honoring Differences

Returning to my 2017 summer in that tranquil nuns' hamlet in El Paso, the afternoon sun still stands out in my memory, filtering through ancient desert willows to paint the ground with patterns of light and shadow. I stood in a circle of nuns and laywomen, preparing for our daily working meditation. Well-worn songbooks were passed around, each page a testament to numerous gatherings like this one.

"Let's sing 'Amazing Grace,'" a nun suggested. As I flipped to the designated page, discomfort descended on me like a fog. The lyrics spoke of sin and redemption, notions that clash with the Buddhist teachings I held dear. When the first notes filled the air, I felt a mild friction between my inner contentment and the song's themes of wretchedness and the need for salvation. I didn't see myself as a sinner in need of rescue; according to Buddha, we are each the architects of our own liberation.

I remembered the song's rich history, written by a white former slave trader turned abolitionist. Yet I couldn't shake the question that loomed in my mind: How far should we go to accommodate different spiritual narratives within a Buddhist framework? While the intent might be inclusivity, the impact felt like a departure from the self-empowered journey central to Buddhist teachings.

One day, I took my concerns to the senior monk at the monastery. "I think it's one thing," I said, "to embrace one another's differences and quite another to keep engaging in activities that feed the ego or singing lyrics that contradict the dharma. Doesn't this go against the Buddha's teachings on not-self and nonattachment?"

The Venerable looked at me with soft eyes and, after a moment of contemplation, said, "This path goes against the stream for many people, especially those who have never been exposed to Buddhism. The majority of Americans were raised with Christian ideals. The principles of not-self, nonattachment, emptiness, and signlessness are foreign to them. But they know love, kindness, generosity, patience. The Buddha taught us to teach the dharma out of compassion and understanding. To create the right conditions for people to be receptive to the dharma, we have to start where they are or at their comfort level. What's more, it is thanks to America and the surrounding community that our monastery is possible. This spiritual life requires mutual support for the purpose of crossing over to the other shore together."

As he spoke, his words seemed to dissolve my rigid perspectives, revealing the nuances I had overlooked.

Nevertheless, when non-Buddhist songs found their way into subsequent work meditation gatherings, I found myself holding back. I kept my mouth closed, my head down, and my eyes focused on the lyrics. While it might have appeared as mere discomfort or stubbornness, my silence was a nuanced form of conscientious objection—a manifestation of my intent to live in accordance with the Buddha's teachings, including the essential principle of wise speech, which advises that our words should echo the depths of our sincere convictions.

My internal struggle isn't an isolated phenomenon; it reflects a broader tension I've noticed within various Buddhist communities. On one hand, some practitioners uphold teachings on not-self and renunciation yet paradoxically cling to lineages and cultural customs as if they were lifelines. On the other, some extol the Buddha's enlightened nature but continue to propagate corrupted scriptures that diminish women and other marginalized communities. This dissonance between proclaimed beliefs and actual practices is not sustainable if we aim to tread the spiritual path with authenticity and integrity.

In America, Buddhism is still taking shape, evolving in its quest for inclusivity and broader appeal. Prominent Buddhist organizations, like the Plum Village Tradition, sometimes risk diluting the essence of the teachings in this process. This tends to occur when Western converts, either from a desire to honor their cultural roots or simply from a lack of awareness, blend Western elements into the practice.

Nevertheless, genuine spiritual growth often comes from stepping out of our comfort zones and diving deep into the teachings as they are, not as we wish them to be. The focus should remain on practices and teachings that resonate with the core principles of Buddhism. This isn't about being exclusionary or narrow-minded; it's about respecting and preserving the authentic wisdom that has the power to liberate each and every one of us.

Cultural Exchange versus Cultural Appropriation

As Buddhism finds its footing in the American landscape, it finds itself dancing on a tightrope between meaningful cultural exchange and potentially harmful cultural appropriation. This challenge presents itself as a delicate seesaw; on one end is the liberating freedom to explore spirituality and on the other, the weighty responsibility to do so in a manner that respects the dignity of marginalized communities.

Cultural appropriation refers to the adoption of elements from another culture, often without understanding or respecting their significance. In the realm of Buddhism, this can manifest in various ways, for instance, businesses like Buddha Bar or Zen Cannabis, which commodify the Buddha's image to sell substances like alcohol and cannabis—products that the Buddha himself would likely reject. These are glaring examples that not only exploit the tradition but also twist its core message.

Conversely, products like Buddha bowls or Tazo Zen Green Tea seem more in tune with what the Buddha talked about, promoting a healthier way of life. Still, the commercialization of these products could dilute the Buddha's teachings into mere buzzwords or fads.

At the heart of it all, I believe the key to responsible engagement with Buddhism—or any spiritual path—comes down to the sincerity of our intent. Diving into Buddhism should be about approaching it with respect, humility, and an earnest hunger to understand its teachings. This makes cultural exchange a beautiful two-way journey: we not only absorb the wisdom of Buddhism but also enrich it by weaving it into fresh, yet respectful, cultural narratives.

Adopting a religion from a culture different from our own is often mistakenly viewed through the lens of cultural appropriation. Yet, as Buddhism finds its footing in the American landscape, it does so as a testament to cultural exchange, not appropriation. Buddhism has always transcended geographical and cultural boundaries, embodying a message of universality rather than exclusivity. Originating in India, it spread across south, southeast, central, and east Asia, eventually landing in the western world. Given its global hopscotch, even I, as a Vietnamese American, could be accused of cultural appropriation from an Indian-rooted faith. But the term *cultural appropriation* doesn't apply here—it's all about the context and the level of respect we bring to the table. After all, the Buddha didn't establish an exclusive community. He discovered a philosophy developed to ease suffering and encouraged his disciples to spread his teachings far and wide.

In modern America, where racial tension is thicker than morning fog, I've seen white practitioners shy away from fully embracing the term *Buddhist*. They're cautious, worried about overstepping some cultural boundaries, choosing instead to stay in their lane. But the thing with Buddhism is that it is all about broadening our lanes, about opening ourselves up to new horizons of understanding and interconnectedness. If we all stuck to what we know, never venturing beyond, what a monochrome world that would be! Instead of staying in our lanes, we should learn to change lanes responsibly, signaling our intentions clearly. In doing so, we're not only enriching our lives but also potentially opening doors for deeper cross-cultural understanding, respect, and unity. And that, in itself, is a step toward easing racial tension.

As Buddhism takes root in the rich soil of American culture, we're standing at a crossroad filled with both promise and pitfalls. While the dharma contains the seeds to bloom into greater inclusivity and equality, unexamined privileges could threaten to choke this promising growth. True progress doesn't come from sitting on the sidelines; it springs from a collective willingness to listen, to learn, and to grow in harmony. Opening our hearts allows for transformative insights that can spread through our communities like pollen on a breeze.

The journey against the stream may be challenging but also wide and welcoming. Our earnest engagement could be the small ripple that evolves into a wave, changing the course of our collective future for the better.

Going Deeper

11

A Critical Examination of Buddhist Schools

After the Buddha's passing, his teachings, once unified, began to diverge as they were passed down orally. This process, like a game of telephone, gave rise to a variety of Buddhist traditions and schools, each blooming in different regions like individual branches sprouting from the same tree.

As we journey into this chapter, it's worth noting that we're entering the final section of the book, aptly named "Going Deeper." Expect this segment to be a more rigorous academic endeavor, enriched with a greater concentration of suttas and deeper analyses of Buddhist thought. Using the EBTs as our guiding star, we'll explore the diverse beliefs and practices of major Buddhist traditions and schools that exist in America today. We'll also continue to ask hard questions, challenge existing norms, and, if necessary, advocate for the removal of practices that don't contribute to our spiritual growth.

The Buddha outlines five benefits of immersing ourselves in the dharma: gaining new knowledge, clarifying what we've learned, dispelling uncertainty, refining our views, and boosting our confidence.[1] As we navigate the pages that follow, my hope is that we'll reap these rewards together.

The Origins and Expansion of Buddhist Schools

The landscape of American Buddhism is nourished by several prominent streams: Theravāda, Mahāyāna, Vajrayāna, and Indo-Tibetan. What you'll find below is a list of various traditions and schools that have blossomed in America, along with their founders wherever traceable.

Note that this list, curated by me, aims to be thorough but is by no means exhaustive. If you notice any omissions, I sincerely apologize and welcome your insights for a more complete picture. Feel free to reach out at contact@kneetran.com. Additionally, you'll observe that this list includes secular and independent movements. Though secular Buddhism receives its own dedicated discussion in chapter 7, its inclusion here adds to the spectrum of understanding that we're aiming to cover.

Theravāda

- Cambodian ថេរវាទ
- Laotian ເຖຣະວາດ
- Myanmarese (Burmese) ထေရဝါဒ
- Sri Lankan ථේරවාදය
  - Mahamevnawa (Kiribathgoda Gnanananda Thero)
- Thai เถรวาท

- Thai Forest Tradition (Ajahn Mun Bhuridatto, Ajahn Chah)
- ✳ Vipassanā
  - American
    - Insight Meditation Center (Howard Nudelman, Ingrid Nudelman, Howard Cohen, Gil Fronsdal)
    - Insight Meditation Community of Washington, DC (Tara Brach)
    - Insight Meditation Society (Sharon Salzberg, Jack Kornfield, Joseph Goldstein)
    - Spirit Rock (Jack Kornfield, Sylvia Boorstein, Anna Douglas, Howard Cohn, James Baraz)
  - Burmese
    - Ba Khin Method (Sayagyi U Ba Khin)
      - S. N. Goenka Method (Burmese Indian Satya Narayana Goenka)
    - New Burmese Method (U Nārada)
      - Mahāsī Method (Mahāsī Sayādaw U Sobhana)
      - Sayadaw Method (Sayadaw U Pandita)
  - Laos
    - Ninayana Buddhism (Thongdee Pongmalee)
  - Sri Lankan
    - Bhavana Society Monastic and Meditation Center (Matthew Flickstein, Bhante Henepola Gunaratana)
  - Thai
    - Wat Buddhawararam of Denver (Achan Sobin S. Namto)

Mahāyāna

- ✳ Humanistic Buddhism or Taiwanese Rénjiān Fójiào (Yin Shun)

        - Chung Tai Shan (Wei Chueh)
        - Dharma Drum Mountain (Sheng Yen)
        - Fo Guang Shan (Hsing Yun)
        - Tzu Chi Foundation (Cheng Yen)
- Nichiren Buddhism or Hokkeshū (Nichiren)
    - Japanese Soka Gakkai International (Daisaku Ikeda)
- Pure Land Buddhism or Jìngtǔzōng (Huiyuan)
    - Korean Jeongto-jong
    - Japanese Jōdo Bukkyō
        - Jōdo Shinshū or Shin Buddhism (Shinran)
            - Buddhist Churches of America
    - Vietnamese Tịnh Độ Tông
- Tiāntāi or Lotus Sūtra School (Zhiyi)
    - Japanese Tendai (Saichō)
    - Korea Cheontae (Uicheon)
- Won Buddhism (Park Chungbin)
- Zen Buddhism
    - Chinese Chán
        - Dharma Realm Buddhist Association (Hsuan Hua)
        - Chán Meditation Society (Sheng Yen)
    - Korean Seon
        - Kwan Um School (Seung Sahn)
        - Taego Order (Taego Bou)
    - Japanese Zen
        - Independent or Beat Zen Movement
            - Beat Zen (Jack Kerouac, Gary Snyder)
        - Rinzai (line of Chinese Linji school, Linji Yixuan)
        - Sanbo Kyodan (Hakuun Yasutani)
            - Buddhist Peace Fellowship (Robert Baker Aitken, Anne Hopkins Aitken, Nelson Foster)

- Sōtō (line of the Chinese Cáodòng school, Dòngshān Liánjiè)
  - San Francisco Zen Center (Shunryu Suzuki Roshi)
- White Plum Asanga (Hakuyu Taizan Maezumi, Taizan Maezumi Roshi)
  - Zen Peacemakers (Bernie Glassman, Sandra Jishu Holmes)

- Vietnamese Thiền
  - Plum Village Tradition and Order of Interbeing (Thích Nhất Hạnh)
  - Bamboo Forest Tradition (Thích Thanh Từ)

Vajrayāna and Indo-Tibetan Buddhism

- Chinese Esotericism
  - True Buddha School or Zhēn Fó Zōng (Lu Sheng-yen)
- Japanese Esotericism
  - Shingon Buddhism (Kūkai)
    - Shinnyo-en (Shinjō Itō, Tomoji)
- Korean Esotericism
  - Jingak Order (Hoedang)
- Indo-Tibetan Buddhism
  - Nyingma School (Padmasambhava, Shantaraksita)
    - Dzogchen (Namkhai Norbu)
    - Rigpa (Sogyal Rinpoche)
  - Kagyu School (Marpa, Milarepa, Gampopa)
    - Diamond Way Buddhism (Danes Hannah Nydahl, Ole Nydahl)
    - Karma Kagyu (Düsum Khyenpa)
    - Barom Kagyu (Barompa Darma Wangchuk)

        - Tshalpa Kagyu (Zhang Yudrakpa Tsöndru Drakpa)
        - Phagdru Kagyu (Phagmo Drupa Dorje)
    - ■ Sakya School (Drogmi)
        - Ngor (Ngorchen Kunga Zangpo)
    - ■ Gelug School (Je Tsongkhapa)
        - Namgyal Monastery Institute of Buddhist Studies (His Holiness the Dalai Lama)
        - Sravasti Abbey (Thubten Chodron)
        - New Kadampa Tradition (Kelsang Gyatso)
        - Foundation for the Preservation of the Mahāyāna Tradition (Thubten Yeshe, Thubten Zopa Rinpoche)
    - ■ Rimé Movement (Jamyang Khyentse Wangpo, Jamgon Kongtrul)
    - ■ Shambhala Buddhism (Chögyam Trungpa)

Independent, Mindfulness, or Secular Movements

- ✳ Independent or Mindfulness Movements
    - ■ American
        - Dialectical Behavior Therapy (Marsha M. Linehan)
        - Interdenominational Buddhism (Dharma Bum Temple, Jeffrey Zlotnik)
        - Mindfulness-Based Stress Reduction (Jon Kabat-Zinn)
        - Unified Mindfulness (Shinzen or Steve Young)
    - ■ English (UK)
        - Triratna Buddhist Community (Sangharakshita)
- ✳ Secular Buddhism
    - ■ Secular Buddhist Association (Ted Meissner)
    - ■ Secular Buddhist Network (founded by a team based primarily in Europe)

- Secular Podcasts
    - Secular Buddhism (Noah Rasheta)
    - The Secular Buddhist (Secular Buddhist Association)
    - Waking Up (Sam Harris)
- ✳ Socially Engaged Buddhism Movement
  - Socially Engaged Buddhism (Robert Aitken, Bernie Glassman)

Theravāda Buddhism

Theravāda, a Pāli term meaning "The Way of the Elders," is the oldest surviving school of Buddhism. It traces its roots back to the Buddha's teachings as preserved in the Pāli Canon, a collection widely regarded as one of the most authentic sources of Buddhist wisdom. Monastics in the Theravāda tradition typically wear robes in shades of burnt orange or maroon, draped around one shoulder, similar to a toga. This is often how the Buddha is portrayed in art and sculpture.

In Theravāda, practitioners aspire to become an *arahant*, or a "perfected person," by following the noble eightfold path. They strive to attain the same enlightenment as the Buddha but without the expectation of teaching the path to others, as a buddha would. The aspiration to become a buddha implies rediscovering the path to enlightenment independently and playing a foundational role in teaching others, a path considered immensely rare and challenging by Theravādins.

Another unique aspect of Theravāda is the reverence for the Abhidhamma Piṭaka as a part of the comprehensive guide toward enlightenment. The Abhidhamma Piṭaka, translating to "higher teaching," is the third and final basket of the Pāli

Canon. It offers an in-depth analysis and systematic arrangement of the Buddha's discourses found in the Sutta Piṭaka, the second basket.

Some Theravādins believe the Abhidhamma Piṭaka was a divine gift from the Buddha to his mother in the heavenly realm of Tavatimsa, later shared with Sāriputta, who then passed it on to his followers. However, modern scholars have suggested that the Abhidhamma Piṭaka was not directly taught by the Buddha but was developed by Buddhist scholars trying to systematize his teachings. As such, it's a later addition to the Pāli Canon and reflects the views of later Buddhist schools rather than the Buddha himself. Despite this, many Theravādins hold the Abhidhamma Piṭaka in high regard, often viewing it as the more advanced teaching and the Buddha's discourses as mere conventional teachings.

The *Jātakas*, or "Past Life Stories of the Buddha," also hold a prominent place in Theravādin literature, though not without controversy. These tales, passed down through various mediums from children's books to high literature, are believed to have been compiled in the third century and heavily influenced by Indian folklore. Some of these stories display blatant misogyny, portraying women as deceptive, evil, and sexually charged. There's a story where the protagonist declares, "Women are wrathful, slanderous, ungrateful . . . sowers of dissension and fierce strife!"[2]

The Ten Perfections, found in the late devotional text, the *Buddhavaṃsa*, also adds to the collection of doctrines that seem out of place. While there's nothing inherently wrong with aspiring to these noble qualities, it's worth noting that they're not found in the EBTs. Yet to some Theravādins, these perfections serve as a roadmap to enlightenment, even though the Buddha's own path to awakening didn't involve ticking off a to-do list.

Then we have the Ten Meritorious Deeds, found in the Abhidhamma. These deeds zero in on themes like charity, merit-making, and reverence, even promoting the idea of "transferring merit to others." While this may seem like a magical quick fix for easing another's struggles, it's at odds with the Buddha's teachings on karma and self-reliance. Imagine trying to pass off our gym workouts to our couch potato friend. As appealing as that might sound to our friend, life doesn't work that way.

To elaborate, this unique concept stems from a tale in the *Stories of Hungry Ghosts*, a late devotional text in the Khuddaka Nikāya, the Minor Collection. Here, the Buddha is said to have told King Bimbisara that merits earned from donations would benefit departed relatives. Yet the Buddha's earliest teachings don't support this claim. He teaches that our actions are the seeds of our destiny: "A doer of good gets good, a doer of bad gets bad."[3] The Buddha emphasizes that our actions are our own, and purity and impurity depend on ourselves; we can't wash away our impurities with someone else's soap.[4] He recognizes that various factors contribute to the conditions of our lives, but the conscious actions we perform through body, speech, and mind are the only things that truly belong to us and follow us like "a shadow that never leaves."[5] So when people attempt to transfer their good karma to others, it's as though they are trying to cheat the system. But karma doesn't play by those rules.

Interestingly, influenced by the Ten Meritorious Deeds, many followers of Theravāda focus heavily on giving gifts, such as food, money, and materials, to the sangha and monastics in an attempt to accumulate merit. While any form of generosity is commendable, it has gotten to the point where this practice has overshadowed the core of Buddhist practice, the noble eightfold path, which the Buddha declares is the path to true merit.[6] Instead of focusing on giving, the Buddha urges us to foster ethical and spiritual growth. He outlines eight ways in which we could earn merit, including taking refuge in the Buddha, dharma, and sangha and observing the five ethical precepts.[7]

Moreover, the Buddha teaches, "Of all the grounds for making worldly merit, none are worth a sixteenth part of the heart's release by love. Surpassing them, the heart's release by love shines and glows and radiates."[8] Here, the Buddha is saying that of all the good things we can do in the world, nothing is as valuable as learning to love. The highest merit comes not from financial offerings or otherworldly acts but from developing pure love and goodwill toward all beings.

The Lay and Monastic Divide

Today's landscape of Theravāda Buddhism, particularly in South Asia, has evolved into a practice that emphasizes devotion. Lay followers primarily play supporting roles, making their offerings and listening with deep reverence to monastic teachings. Monks, on the other hand, have taken the center stage as the primary educators, interpreters, and practitioners of the dharma.

In 2016, I found myself surrounded by the natural beauty of Oregon, immersed in the practice of Theravāda Buddhism as a weekend retreatant at a hermitage. The reverence the laypeople showered on the monks was a sight to behold, a notch above what I'd become accustomed to in Mahāyāna settings. The atmosphere was imbued with a unique, respectful silence: soft-spoken conversations, downcast eyes, and hands coming together in a bow whenever a monk passed by. The monks were the first to serve themselves during meals, and as they claimed their seats on elevated platforms during dharma talk sessions, the laypeople remained seated on the floor, their sense of deference and devotion palpable.

My younger sister, who joined me, remarked on the air of superiority the monks seemed to project. And in her characteristic frankness, she said, "And you know how I feel about that." In other words, it bothered her. But it wasn't just the power dynamics that left a lingering discomfort. During the Q&A session, one monk was fighting off sleep, while others gave answers that felt disconnected from the essence of the Buddha's teachings, failing to inspire us.

For example, when someone asked how to break free from the habit of comparing themselves with others, a monk responded, "What's wrong with comparing?" Then he proceeded to justify the practice of comparison, arguing that it could spur improvement and learning.

This response seemed at odds with the Buddha's teachings, which encourage us to reflect on our actions instead of focusing on others.[9] He says that comparing and judging can open the door to jealousy, setting us up for a landslide of violence, hostility, and hatred. The way to free ourselves from these harmful states is to understand their roots in our thoughts and our sense of self.[10]

As I pondered on this, I realized that not all retreat participants might have the luxury of time or resources to dive deep into the dharma. They would likely accept the monks' words as truth, a trend rooted deeply in the history of Buddhism.

Yet this historical tendency contrasts sharply with the Buddha's original vision as recorded in the EBTs. He envisioned a community where monks, nuns, and laypeople were not passive recipients but active, knowledgeable, and consistent practitioners. He saw everyone as potential teachers, clarifiers, analyzers, and torchbearers of his teachings.[11]

The Buddha paved the path for ordinary people like you and me who seek wisdom and peace and yearn to help others do the same. A true follower isn't a passive listener but actively upholds faith, ethical conduct, and generosity while guiding others in these virtues. Such a person is continually willing to learn, reflect, and integrate the teachings into everyday life.[12]

The story of Citta, an ordinary layman, serves as a reminder of this. He enlightened several monks that neither the sense organs (like the eye) nor their objects (like sights) are the fetters themselves; rather, the fetter is the desire and greed that arise from their interaction.[13] His wisdom was so noteworthy that the Buddha himself praised him, declaring Citta the foremost dharma speaker among his lay disciples. This story shows that lay followers are fully capable of not just practicing the dharma but also guiding others in it—even monastics—when the situation calls for it.

In our modern world, monastics are often seen as superior beings, creating feelings of superiority among monastics and inferiority among lay followers. But as we've explored in earlier chapters, the Buddha warns us against viewing ourselves as superior, inferior, or even equal to others. These are three toxic mindsets that distort our relationships and our own self-view. He stresses that donning a saffron robe doesn't elevate one to a higher pedestal, much like slapping frosting on a cake doesn't guarantee it will taste good. Just as the real flavor of a cake comes from its ingredients and how they're mixed and baked, true spiritual stature comes from one's actions, thoughts, and inner qualities—not the outer trappings of religious life.

In fact, the Buddha warns against monastics who cling to negative tendencies like greed, arrogance, stinginess, and dishonesty, saying, "They don't deserve the label 'outer robe wearer' just because they wear an outer robe."[14]

These words ring true when we come across disturbing revelations about some monastics' lifestyles. The Theravāda tradition, which prides itself on its strict adherence to rules that govern the conduct of monastics, is not immune to human flaws.

For instance, in Thailand, over 50 percent of health problems diagnosed among Buddhist monks are smoking-related. In 2022, a Thai temple lost all four of its resident monks to rehab centers due to meth use. In Cambodia, one in three monks is a smoker, while in Sri Lanka, monks are allowed to chew tobacco—a habit as addictive and destructive as smoking.

The Buddha would have been deeply troubled by these behaviors. In one sutta, he expressed disappointment at monks who seemed restless and heedless, their minds wandering aimlessly, and their tongues running loose. He emphasizes the dangers of straying from the spiritual path. Neglecting self-control and falling into states of dullness and drowsiness, he warns, put one at risk of negative influences and self-destructive behaviors.[15]

The Buddha teaches that bodily consumption should be solely to sustain the body, to avoid harm, and to support spiritual practice, "not for fun, indulgence, adornment, or decoration."[16] He advises his followers to avoid stockpiling goods for their personal pleasure[17] and suggests that they should instead find true joy in quenching the flames of craving.[18]

Caste Discrimination Defies the Buddha's Teachings

Another example where actual practice diverges from the Buddha's teachings is the ongoing caste-based ordination system in Sri Lanka's Siam Nikaya. This prominent monastic order restricts high-level ordination to only the radala and govigama castes. Such a practice stands in stark contrast to the Buddha's teachings, which emphasizes inner virtue over external attributes like caste or financial status.

The Buddha taught that the real measure of a person lies in their actions, their wisdom, their principles, and their moral conduct—not their family line or wealth.[19] He opened the doors of his sangha to everyone, irrespective of their social standing, affirming that anyone willing to put forth the effort could achieve ultimate purity.[20]

In a conversation with King Pasenadi of Kosala, the Buddha used the analogy of different types of wood used to kindle fires, saying that the fire—akin to enlightenment—remains the same regardless of the wood, or caste, from which it originates.[21]

Against this backdrop of the Buddha's inclusivity, it's notable that as recently as 2023, Seattle became the first US city to ban caste discrimination. The need for such a legislation in a city known for its diverse and progressive views underlines the stubborn persistence of caste prejudices. The enduring presence of the caste system in Sri Lanka and other countries demonstrates how these societal norms, deeply ingrained over centuries, travel across oceans and take root in new countries—indicating how difficult it is to bring beliefs and actions into alignment.

Soon after Seattle's move, California enacted the California Civil Rights Act of 2023, which was signed into law on

September 28, 2023. This landmark legislation, the first of its kind at the state level in the United States, expands antidiscrimination protections to include caste. As the law prepares to go into effect on January 1, 2024, there is hopeful anticipation that it will inspire broader change across the nation.

The Struggle for Gender Equality and Inclusion

The landscape of Theravāda Buddhism has been marked by significant gender disparities. Despite the Buddha's teachings that inner qualities and actions define a person, some in the community ignore his guidance on the subject, adhering to antiquated and groundless rules that continue to marginalize women.

In several Theravāda countries, a supreme patriarch, or *sangharaja*—appointed by the state—governs the monastics. In Thailand, for example, the king selects the sangharaja, who then exercises authority over Theravāda and a small fraction of Mahāyāna Buddhists. This sangharaja also heads the Sangha Supreme Council, the sole authority to conduct monastic ordinations. However, this centralized, hierarchical model of governance varies from the Buddha's original teachings, which encouraged a more collective decision-making process among monastics to mitigate the concentration of power on any single individual.

As the Buddha neared his final moments, Ānanda, filled with trepidation, asked about the future of the sangha and the Buddha's expectations. The Buddha advises that reliance should be on oneself and the dharma—rather than on a single leader. He essentially articulates, "Whether I'm here or have passed away, those who live as their own island, their own refuge, with no other refuge, and who take the teaching as their island and their refuge, with no other refuge, shall be among the best of the best."[22]

The Buddha also warns against the pursuit of fame, status, and control over monasteries. He asserts that such desires often lead to harmful consequences, like fanning the flames of greed and pride, leading one astray.[23] Extending this warning to monastics' interactions with royalty and political affairs, he advises restraint in frequent visits to royal courts as it could foster misunderstandings about undue influence.[24] During an occasion when a group of monastics gathered in an assembly hall, engaging in discourse about the wealth, forces, and power of various kings, the Buddha sternly reminds them, "It is not appropriate for you who have chosen the path of renunciation to talk about such things. When you're sitting together, you should do one of two things: discuss the teachings or maintain noble silence."[25]

In the Buddha's time, ordination was a simple affair, devoid of elaborate ceremonies. Anyone with a sincere desire to lead a monastic life could join the sangha. The Buddha and his disciples—monks and nuns alike—welcomed new members with open arms, often with a warm "come, mendicant!"[26] At times, the Buddha personalized this invitation, like when he welcomed the nun Bhaddā with "come, Bhaddā!"[27] This period in history marked the Buddha's sangha as a sanctuary of equality and inclusivity, with nuns as integral members.

However, fast-forward to the present day, and the picture is strikingly different. Formalities have taken center stage, and the ordination process has grown complicated and ceremonious. More alarmingly, the ordination of women has dwindled, if not completely ceased, in many parts of the world. Such a shift raises concerns about how far modern Theravāda communities have strayed from the Buddha's open-door policy.

To grasp the scope of this issue, let's take a quick globetrotting tour. In Myanmar, a 1981 policy effectively barred women from achieving full ordination as nuns. In Thailand, a 1928 law once created similar roadblocks, and although this law was lifted in 2002, the two major Theravāda orders within the country still don't officially recognize fully ordained nuns. This disheartening pattern is also visible in Cambodia, Sri Lanka, and Laos.

These modern policies are inconsistent with history. Nuns were once the beating heart of Theravāda Buddhism. They remained an integral part until the eleventh century in Sri Lanka, the thirteenth century in Burma, the fourteenth century in Thailand, the eighteenth century in Cambodia, and the twentieth century in Laos. Various calamities like wars and famines reportedly led to the loss of the bhikkhuni lineage. And while those grim days are behind us, most Theravāda sanghas continue to deny nun ordinations, insisting on a groundless rule that mandates the presence of both nun and monk orders to validate any nun ordination. They hold that without existing nuns in their tradition, new nun ordinations are impossible.

When Mahāyāna nuns extended a helping hand, the offer was declined, citing that accepting ordination from another tradition would disrupt their lineage and cause disagreements over beliefs and monastic disciplines.

In defiance of these challenges, a wave of Sri Lankan female aspirants, backed by Mahāyāna Taiwanese and Korean monastics, achieved full ordination in the late '80s and mid-'90s. Among these trailblazers was Bhikkhuni Kusuma. Even in the face of potential backlash from local authorities, she conducted secret nun ordination ceremonies, ultimately revitalizing the bhikkhuni order in Sri Lanka. In a 2018 interview, Kusuma shared, "We now have about 3,000 bhikkhunis, and it was after my first ordination that the word *bhikkhuni* was once again known and heard in Sri Lanka!"

Further afield, in 2009, British-born monk Ajahn Brahm and his disciple Bhante Sujato conducted the first full nun ordination in western Australia, supported by an international group of eight nuns. Despite facing expulsion from his sangha and a ban from the Ajahn Chah tradition afterward, Venerable Ajahn Brahm remained steadfast in his conviction. His loyalty, he declared, was to the teachings of the dharma and Vinaya, not the Thai state.

Over the last decade, there's been a wave of Theravāda nun ordinations across the globe, from the United States to Germany and Indonesia, and even in traditional Theravāda countries. While resistance still exists among some Theravāda monks, a division has emerged within the community, fueling ongoing debates on the legitimacy of female ordinations.

In chapter 5, we delved into the *Gotamī Sutta* and its problematic "eight rules of respect," which have acted as roadblocks to women's inclusion in Theravāda traditions. Rule six, in particular, requires that a novice nun must seek ordination from both monk and nun communities after practicing for two years—a requirement that seems inapplicable in the context of Gotamī's immediate ordination. After all, Gotamī was ordained immediately after accepting these rules, without the two-year novitiate and at a time when there was no established nun community to endorse her.

This discrepancy compels us to ask: How could the Buddha, the epitome of insight, impose a two-year training period and an ordination process reliant on an order of nuns that did not yet exist? It seems paradoxical for the Buddha to set forth a condition that could not have been fulfilled by Gotamī herself. Furthermore, why establish such prerequisites when he himself allowed for an ordination devoid of these obstacles? This leads to another critical inquiry: Why are modern Buddhist communities so fixated on maintaining ordination lineages?

The Buddha once compared the belief in a lineage of teachers to a line of blind men, each one blindly following the one in front, stepping into uncertainty without personal discernment.[28] He also advised a young Brahmin named Kesamutti not to rely on lineage or tradition but on personal experience and understanding.[29]

This wisdom resonates deeply when we consider the stories of empowered nuns like Soṇā,[30] Uttamā,[31] Vijayā,[32] Uttarāta,[33] and Sukkā,[34] among thirty others.[35] These nuns received ordination without the need for monks or the presence of the Buddha himself, underscoring the Buddha's encouragement for his followers to trust their own judgment and authority in spiritual matters.

Yet, despite such empowering examples set by the Buddha, it's both surprising and ironic that the "Way of the Elders" tradition has veered off course. Instead of staying true to the Buddha's teachings, this tradition has been swayed by a variety of influences, including the whims of various leaders and heads of governments.

It's worth noting that no single tradition today can claim sectarian purity in Buddhism. We're all branches of the same family tree, our roots reaching back to the Buddha himself. The journey to enlightenment isn't about following in the footsteps of the elders; it's about forging our own path, guided by the dharma—the original teachings of the Buddha.

This emphasis on lineage also clashes with the Buddha's teachings on not-self and nonattachment. It's like building a wall around one's ego, a self-identity that the Buddha encourages us to dismantle on our journey toward liberation. He says that truly understanding form leads us to realize "this is not mine, I am not this, this is not myself," liberating us from attachment.[36]

Verses from the *Dhammapada* further reinforce this point: "Suffering won't torment the one who has nothing, not clinging to name and form."[37]

In another discourse, the Buddha elaborates on the theme of nonattachment to identity while still engaging with the conventional world:

> Someone who has given up conceit has no ties,
> the ties of conceit are all dissipated.
> Though that clever person has transcended identity,
> they'd still say, "I speak,"
> and also "they speak to me."
> Skilled and understanding the world's conventions,
> they'd use these terms as no more than expressions.[38]

Considering the principle of inclusivity, the Buddha identifies four pillars that define a noble disciple: wisdom, energy, blamelessness, and inclusiveness. He asserts that some people who do not include others might fear disrepute—that is, being held in low esteem by the public—but a noble disciple possessing these four strengths would have no such fear.[39] In other words, a noble disciple of the Buddha wouldn't yield to societal norms or pressures that contradict these cornerstones. They would remain steadfast in their commitment to uphold the Buddha's teachings in their entirety—including the principle of inclusiveness.

In many Theravāda monasteries, it's common to see nuns with shaved heads, donning white or pink robes. But their status is kind of in limbo, existing in a space somewhere between laypeople and fully ordained monastics. With inadequate training or financial support, they're often relegated to menial tasks like sweeping, cooking, and doing laundry. Their status is generally perceived as secondary, even compared with the most junior monks, no matter their age, wisdom, or accomplishments.

This reality contrasts significantly with the Buddha's original vision for his community. He once said, "These four competent, educated, assured, learned people—who have memorized the teachings and practice in line with the teachings—beautify the Saṅgha. What four? A monk, a nun, a layman, and a laywoman."[40]

This sentiment, echoed in countless EBTs, underscores that nuns were indispensable to the Buddha's spiritual community. For those in the Theravāda tradition who aspire to tread in the Buddha's footsteps, embracing the full participation of women in the sangha should be a natural step. Holding on to notions of sectarian purity, legalism, or any other rationale opposing the inclusion of women is like erecting a giant flashing billboard of discrimination that defies the Buddha's teachings. Promoting inclusivity and empowering women not only strengthen the sangha but also pave the way toward a more compassionate and equitable world. It's time to bring these invisible nuns out of the shadows and into the light, where they belong.

Mahāyāna Buddhism

The Sanskrit term *mahāyāna* translates to "great vehicle." We can picture it as a cosmic shuttle, offering everyone a ride to nirvāṇa, regardless of their ability to foot the bill. At the heart of this tradition is the concept of a *bodhisattva*, a spiritual seeker committed to delaying their personal enlightenment until every sentient being has been liberated from the clutches of suffering. To Mahāyānists, the bodhisattva path is a selfless and compassionate journey dedicated to the well-being of others.

This grand aspiration, however, has led some Mahāyānists to label Theravāda as *hīnayāna*—a Sanskrit term meaning "lesser vehicle." This is because Theravāda is often seen as focusing on individual enlightenment. But let's clear up a misunderstanding here.

While it's true that Theravāda does emphasize personal enlightenment, this focus is not at the expense of the welfare of others. In fact, many Theravādins are deeply committed to contributing to the betterment of society. They take inspiration from the Buddha himself, who dedicated forty-five years after his own enlightenment to teaching and uplifting others.

Consider the likes of Ajahn Buddhadāsa, Walpola Rahula, and Shravasti Dhammika, monastics who have been instrumental in bringing the dharma to Western shores. Or reflect on the life of Dhammananda Bhikkhuni, a pioneering force in the struggle for female ordination in Thailand and Asia, who earned a place in the BBC's 2019 list of the hundred most influential and inspiring women globally.

My personal journey with the dharma has been immeasurably enriched by Theravāda monastics like Bhikkhu Bodhi, Ayya Khemā, Bhikkhu Anālayo, and Bhante Sujato. Their writings and translations have deepened my understanding of the dharma and inspired me to speak my mind and my truth, even when it's not easy.

In the journey of Buddhism, compassion and wisdom are like two wings of a bird, working in harmony to maintain balance. They capture the essence of this spiritual path: a deep compassion for others' suffering, coupled with the wisdom to understand our minds, reality, and our shared experiences of suffering. No matter the tradition, these qualities are fundamental to all Buddhists. Personal enlightenment and societal well-being are not mutually exclusive but are often interwoven in the lives and practices of its followers.

As a matter of fact, despite being aware of Mahāyāna sūtras that criticize the arahant path and non-Mahāyanists, Theravādins have shown remarkable compassion. They have chosen not to retaliate, their texts devoid of any harsh criticisms of Mahāyāna. Even with a general dismissal of Mahāyāna texts as later additions and the multitude of buddhas and bodhisattvas that they introduce, Theravādins have faithfully upheld the Buddha's teachings on wise speech and social harmony.

A Landscape of Diverse Traditions and Texts

It has been established that Mahāyāna sūtras' divergence from early Buddhism presents unique challenges to this school of thought. While within the school, there exist traditions that engage with EBTs, such as the Chinese Āgamas, which parallels the early Pāli Canon, the boarder Mahāyāna philosophy is far more eclectic. This school is characterized by its experiential, flexible, and adaptable nature, drawing from a broad array of sources. Such a broad scope has led to numerous Mahāyāna subschools, each with its own set of revered texts, interpretations, practices, and unique buddhas and bodhisattvas. Even the monastic attire in Mahāyāna traditions serves as a testimony to its diversity, ranging from formal robes in shades of gray, yellow, black, or brown, often accessorized with ceremonial sashes or hats.

Delving deeper into this complexity, consider the staggering variety within Mahāyāna. Pure Land Buddhism revolves around three main texts: the *Longer Splendor of the Blissful Land Sūtra,* the *Shorter Splendor of the Blissful Land Sūtra*, and the *Contemplation on Amitāyus Sūtra.*

Nichiren Buddhism, on the other hand, focuses largely on the *Lotus Sūtra* and Nichiren's own writings.

Schools like Shinnyo-en Buddhism, Tiāntāi, and Tzu Chi each bring its own texts to the table, including, in Tzu Chi's case, its founders' own ten precepts.

And then there's Zen, which gives a nod to a variety of texts but also emphasizes direct experience over scriptural study, suggesting that enlightenment can be attained without the aid of written teachings.

With so many schools, so many texts to choose from, it can feel like a classroom where every student writes their own textbook. Every narrative has its angle; each angle claims to be the right one. This bewildering diversity can make it challenging for followers to discern the authenticity of all these texts, especially given that many Mahāyāna sūtras aren't universally accepted as the Buddha's teachings.

Between Devotion and Critical Inquiry

Introspection and critical examination are essential to all Buddhist traditions, but Mahāyāna faces a unique challenge in this regard. Many Mahāyāna sūtras act like enthusiastic cheerleaders for their own team, singing praises of their own path and teachings. But their cheerleading doesn't stop at mere self-promotion—they also play defense, issuing stern warnings against those who dare to criticize or belittle them.

Take, for instance, the *Lotus Sūtra*. It presents itself as the "king of sūtras" and cautions of dire consequences for those who dare to speak ill of its practitioners, asserting that such criticisms would destroy all their prospects of achieving buddhahood in this lifetime.

Similarly, the *Great Nirvāṇa Sūtra* parades itself as superior to all sūtras, comparing itself to milk as the finest of all tastes. It praises the great bodhisattvas who, "having gained life as men," upheld and protected the wisdom of Mahāyāna Buddhism and defeated "people of other teachings" who opposed the "Wonderful Dharma."

Similarly, the *Contemplation on Amitāyus Sūtra* suggests that if we've committed some evil deeds, we can still earn good karma by refraining from speaking ill of Mahāyāna sūtras.

Meanwhile, the *Shorter Splendor of the Blissful Land Sūtra* urges us to trust and believe in its words, claiming they're the genuine teachings "truly spoken by all buddhas."

This pattern of self-endorsement contrasts with the ethos found in the EBTs, where the Buddha himself discourages self-glorification[41] and urges a personal and rigorous investigation of his teachings. He advises us to keep our eyes open, to question what we see, and to test what we hear.[42] He prompts us to embrace teachings that are beneficial, relevant, and immediately effective[43]—those that invite examination[44] and can endure critical evaluation.[45] The enthusiastic self-praise present in the Mahāyāna sūtras, then, suggests a hint of insecurity, as if they're trying to convince themselves as much as their readers.

Nevertheless, many Mahāyāna practitioners, perhaps out of respect for and deference to authority, tend to shy away from questioning these texts. They lean toward familiar practices like chanting sūtras or meditation. And while these practices offer comfort, by not critically examining their own sūtras in light of early texts, they risk missing the full depth of Buddhism. It's like having a toolbox but only ever using a hammer. Over time, this could lead to a sense of stagnation, curtailing the potential rewards of spiritual pursuits and possibly leading to a diminishing interest in Buddhism altogether.

The Waning Popularity of Buddhism

This declining trend is mirrored in data from the Pew Research Center. In 2010, Buddhists made up 7 percent of the global population—a decent slice of the spiritual pie. But by 2050, though the total population is projected to grow, the proportion of Buddhists might shrink to 5 percent. It's as if we're watching our piece of pie get smaller while the pie itself gets bigger.

This downslide is particularly noticeable in the Asia-Pacific region, home to a significant portion of the world's Buddhists. Even as the region's overall population is expected to surge by 22 percent, the Buddhist population is projected to decline by 15 percent.

Focusing on specific countries, in predominantly Mahāyāna nations such as China, Japan, Malaysia, South Korea, and Việt Nam, Japan led in 2010, with 36 percent identifying as Buddhists. By 2050, however, Japan is set to witness an 11 percent drop, the most significant decline among these countries.

Conversely, in countries predominantly following the Theravāda tradition, like Myanmar, Sri Lanka, and Thailand, despite often being labeled as the "lesser vehicle," these nations have a considerably larger percentage of their population identifying as Buddhists than the Mahāyāna countries, with Cambodia leading at a striking 97 percent. Yet, similar to the Mahāyāna countries, these Theravāda nations are projected to see a decrease in the share of Buddhists by 2050. However, these decreases are less severe than those projected for Mahāyāna countries, averaging 1.5 percent compared with 4.6 percent.

The factors driving these shifts are multifaceted. Demographic trends play a significant role—Buddhists tend to have aging populations and lower fertility rates. Additionally, individuals are converting to other religions, such as Christianity or Islam, due to factors ranging from missionary activity to the perceived benefits of these other faiths. For Mahāyāna countries, however, a significant factor is the complexity and diversity of Mahāyāna practices. With its multiple buddhas, bodhisattvas, superstitions, and rituals, Mahāyāna Buddhism has moved somewhat away from the Buddha's original teachings, making it less appealing and accessible to some.

In the United States, despite projections pointing to an increase in the share of Buddhists by 2050, reaching up to about 6.1 million people, or a 1.4 percent increase, it's essential to distinguish the source of this growth. It seems that this surge is fueled by more secular forms of Buddhism—in mindfulness, vipassanā, and other independent movements that ground themselves in the Buddha's teachings on meditation and ethics and don't rely heavily on supernatural elements. Notably, a 2023 Pew Research Study underscores a subtle decline among Asian Americans identifying with Buddhism—from 14 percent in 2012 to 11 percent in 2023. This decline is pronounced among large US ethnic groups such as Chinese, Korean, Vietnamese, and

Japanese—all with ancestral roots in countries where Mahāyāna Buddhism is the predominant tradition. This data suggests that while Buddhism, especially its secular forms, may be gaining traction among convert Buddhists in the United States, traditional Mahāyāna Buddhism, especially among Asian Americans, sees a concerning decline.

The Buddha's Emphasis on Wisdom

The Buddha taught the greatest gift we can offer is the gift of wisdom.[46] The best form of compassionate speech is to teach dharma to those who are engaged and willing to listen, and the most effective way to care for another is to instill faith in the faithless, ethics in the unethical, generosity in the stingy, and wisdom in the ignorant.[47]

Yet many Mahāyāna traditions today primarily encourage followers to pray to the Buddha and other deities for help or to spend hours chanting and sitting in meditation—painful or not—without any tangible payoff. It makes us wonder, what's the point of following the Buddha if we don't study his teachings?

Once, a nun from the Plum Village Tradition shared with me that she only read books by her teacher, Zen Master Thích Nhất Hạnh, because they taught her everything she needed to know about Buddhism. And I remember nodding, understanding her perspective, having myself read nearly fifty of his books. However, by focusing only on his works, we risk missing out on the treasure that lies within the EBTs. Despite Thích Nhất Hạnh being one of the few Mahāyāna teachers who studied the Pāli Canon and integrated many of its key principles into his tradition, depending exclusively on his interpretations is like choosing an apprentice over the master himself.

Just as a lotus needs its roots and mud to produce stems, leaves, flowers, and seeds, so do all schools of Buddhism, including Theravāda, Mahāyāna, Vajrayāna, Indo-Tibetan, and secular, depend on the EBTs. For the Mahāyāna tradition to regain trust of its followers, it must be willing to take a good, hard look at itself, critically examine its beliefs and practices, and be ready to change when necessary to confront the challenges they face. This includes tackling cultural biases, addressing inequalities and superstitions, and ensuring that the teachings are accessible, practical, and rooted in the Buddha's original teachings. This becomes particularly essential in Western societies, where values like rational thinking, independence, and gender equality hold sway, where skepticism toward anything that appears mythical is commonplace, and where a level of scientific literacy is generally expected.

Even the Buddha himself warns against distorting his teachings, noting that such actions could harm others and cause the true teachings to disappear. He states, "By memorizing the discourses incorrectly, taking only a semblance of the phrasing, some mendicants shut out the meaning and the teaching. They act for the hurt and unhappiness of the people, for the harm and suffering of many people. . . . They make the true teaching disappear."[48]

Rituals and Modern Mahāyāna Practices

One intriguing aspect of Mahāyāna Buddhism is the idea that hierarchy, strict discipline, rituals, and formal procedures are all part and parcel of the spiritual journey. Certain Zen schools, for example, view this tough discipline as the gateway to transformation, a path to freedom from our egos and delusion. They argue that spending hours in meditation, wrestling with fatigue, engaging in Eastern rituals, and puzzling over cryptic koans are all part of the quest for peace in the whirlwind of life's toughest storms. The premise is that if we can handle these discomforts, then we can handle anything life hurls our way.

But wait, didn't the Buddha advocate for the middle way—a balanced approach that avoids both extreme indulgence and harsh austerity? He himself had tried out some intense ascetic practices in his own journey before realizing they didn't bring him closer to enlightenment.

The Buddha teaches that self-inflicted suffering is not only painful but also counterproductive. Such practices could perpetuate harm, stress, and illness.[49] He points out that those who adhere strictly to rules and regulations and harsh self-mortification could keep at it for a hundred years, but they'd still find their minds in chains.[50]

In one sutta, the Buddha breaks down four distinct "lanes" of spiritual practice, each with its own set of perks and pitfalls. Imagine we're at a spiritual buffet: the first lane is like grabbing all the sugary desserts—we enjoy the sweetness now but deal with a bellyache later. These are practices that feel great in the moment but end up backfiring, often because they're all about chasing immediate thrills without considering the consequences.

The second lane is like eating bread that has gone bad—unpleasant now, and we'll regret it later. These are the practices where we might push ourselves too hard physically and emotionally, but instead of leading us toward enlightenment, they end up causing more suffering in the long run.

Now, the third lane is like eating our veggies—we might not love it, but it's beneficial in the long run. These are practices that may be challenging in the short term, but they're setting us up for significant spiritual growth.

The fourth lane, however, is the path the Buddha holds as ideal. It's the balanced meal— the sweet spot—the perfectly seasoned main course that satisfies now and nourishes for the long haul. These are the practices that provide immediate contentment and laying the foundation for lasting spiritual well-being. Think of them as the golden mean between self-indulgence and self-denial.[51]

When we approach sitting meditation, it's helpful to think of it as a spa day for our minds. Meditation is a practice of scrubbing away mental impurities and nurturing contentment, compassion, and wisdom. Instead of plunging into extreme practices to overcome our ego, attachments, and arrogance, we can do it through meditation that focuses on the concepts of signlessness[52] and not-self.[53]

In Buddhism, signlessness is about recognizing there's no permanent, unchanging self. By understanding that everything, including us, is in a constant state of flux, we can open up our hearts and clear away the clutter of greed and ill will, and make room for clarity and understanding. When we see reality as it really is—impermanent and ever-changing—we no longer feel the need to cling to our identity, doubt our own abilities, or feel unduly attached to the rules and traditions we've been taught.[54] Instead, we can navigate life with a sense of freedom and flexibility, adapting to changes as they come without losing our inner peace.

The concept of not-self encourages us to let go of our strong identification with any form, whether thoughts, feelings, perceptions, or our physical bodies. The goal is to understand that there's no separate, stand-alone "I" that exists independent of the rest of the universe. It's like realizing we're not solitary islands in the ocean but part of the vast sea itself.

The Buddha suggests that when we meditate with this concept of not-self in mind, we can begin to dismantle that sense of "I-making, mine-making, and conceit." This kind of transformation in our awareness can help us transcend the usual boundaries of discrimination and self-centeredness, leading us to a place of peace, freedom, and profound connection with all of life.[55]

Consider the time when the Buddha encountered a householder named Sigālaka who was engrossed in ritual behavior of reverence toward the six directions—east, south, west, north, below, and above. Sensing an opportunity, the Buddha proposed a more enriching alternative. He encouraged Sigālaka to direct his dedication toward nurturing six essential relationships: those with teachers, parents, spouses, friends, coworkers, and spiritual guides. Moreover, he advised against four destructive behaviors and warned him of certain habits and actions that could jeopardize his well-being.[56]

This encounter highlights the Buddha's belief that an overreliance on rituals and rules can hinder genuine spiritual progress.[57] Yet fast-forward to today, and we find that rituals have woven themselves deeply into certain Mahāyāna traditions. While some ceremonies embody the essence of Buddhism—such as expressing parental respect by wearing red or white roses at the Ullambana Festival—there are others that may diverge from the Buddha's original teachings.

Take, for example, the elaborate ceremonies dedicated to deceased ancestors that sometimes unfold in certain communities. While Buddhism honors the idea of ancestor respect, the Buddha's own days were steeped in simplicity.

The use of amulets and talismans is another area where cultural practices may have distanced themselves from the core of Buddhist teachings. Though these items are often revered as protective or lucky, the Buddha emphasized the impermanence of material possessions and the futility of seeking external solutions to internal challenges.

Last but not least, the hierarchical practices seen in some schools can contradict the egalitarian spirit that the Buddha endorsed. Whether in the form of special statuses within the spiritual community or rigid layers of authority, these hierarchies can cloud the Buddhist teachings on egolessness and equality, deviating from the direct path to liberation that the Buddha illuminated.

While traditions and rituals can serve as touchstones of faith and community, it's important to discern which practices genuinely align with the essence of Buddhism and which might veer us off the path. The Buddha's own lifestyle—rooted in meditation, simplicity, and ethical and compassionate conduct—serves as a gold standard for assessing the value of today's practices.

If we contrast the Buddha's lifestyle with the wide array of practices, formalities, and rituals that Buddhism has accumulated over centuries, we might wonder: Would the Buddha himself be surprised by such complexities? This contrast is like comparing a calm, peaceful walk in the park with the energetic buzz of a carnival—both have their charm, but they offer different vibes.

Every now and then, it's worthwhile to pause, reflect, and ask: Which of these two experiences resonates more with our own spiritual goals? How can we shape our individual paths to reflect the true essence of Buddhism?

Vajrayāna and Indo-Tibetan Buddhism

In the West, particularly in America, the terms *Vajrayāna* and *Indo-Tibetan Buddhism* are often used interchangeably. However, these two forms of Mahāyāna Buddhism have unique origins, practices, and teachings, even though they're interconnected in many ways.

Indo-Tibetan Buddhism is a fusion of Vajrayāna elements, Indian Mahāyāna Buddhist philosophy, and ancient Tibetan customs. Its distinct subschools, such as Nyingma, Kagyu, Sakya, and Gelug, have each contributed a distinct blend of teachings, texts, and practices within this tradition. Monastics in this tradition generally wear robes of deep maroon or burgundy, sometimes complemented by a golden-yellow shawl or sash.

Vajrayāna Buddhism, also known as the "Diamond Vehicle" or the "Thunderbolt Vehicle," initially emerged in India around the fifth century. The term *Vajrayāna* derives from the vajra, a mythical weapon of the god Indra that represents its invincible and potent qualities—indestructible like a diamond and powerful like thunder. This name reflects the Vajrayāna approach to enlightenment—firm, unwavering, and potent.

Unlike other Buddhist schools, Vajrayāna integrates specialized practices using mantras, mudras, and mandalas, coupled with advanced yoga and meditations on deities, to accelerate one's path to enlightenment. This esoteric tradition would later spread to Tibet in the seventh century under King Songtsen Gampo. Intent on establishing Buddhism as a state religion, Gampo invited scholars from India and China, including the Indian tantric master Padmasambhava, to plant seeds of

Vajrayāna in Tibetan soil. By the end of his reign, Buddhism had become Tibet's state religion.

Vajrayāna's entry into Tibet led to a unique interplay with existing Mahāyāna philosophies and local Tibetan customs, laying the foundation for what we now refer to as Indo-Tibetan Buddhism. In the fourteenth century, Tibetan scholar Butön Rinchen Drub took a pivotal step by compiling the Kangyur and Tengyur. The Kangyur features a mix of Mahāyāna texts, Vajrayāna tantras, and Nyingma tantras, with only a quarter of these stemming from the Pāli Canon. The Tengyur is a compilation of commentaries and treatises by Indian authors. Together, they form the Tibetan Buddhist Canon—a unique body of scripture that some view as a deviation from the Buddha's original teachings.

As of 2023, only a quarter of the Kangyur and a part of the Tengyur have been translated into English. This language gap often necessitates a reliance on Tibetan teachers for interpretation, creating an additional hurdle for non-Tibetan scholars and practitioners.

At the heart of Indo-Tibetan Buddhism lies a distinct tradition—the Tülku system—that identifies reincarnated spiritual leaders who guide monastic communities from a young age. This system has played a pivotal role in preserving Tibetan Buddhism through political instability and cultural suppression. However, it has also amplified some voices while silencing others, with women particularly feeling this disparity.

Perhaps you've heard of Pema Chödrön and Thubten Chodron, two prominent nuns associated with Tibetan Buddhism in the West. It's worth bearing in mind that their ordination hails from East Asia Mahāyāna traditions, not Indo-Tibetan. This is because, historically, Indo-Tibetan Buddhism has not permitted women to receive full ordination, limiting their access to higher studies and positions of influence.

Against this backdrop of inequality, there's a growing movement striving for change. Key figures like the Dalai Lama and His Holiness the 17th Gyalwang Karmapa—head of the Karma Kagyu Lineage—have been vocal advocates for the full ordination of women in Indo-Tibetan Buddhism. However, their calls have yet to translate into tangible actions within their communities, primarily due to resistance from male monastics in their orders.

In contrast to these challenges, the year 2022 emerged as a watershed moment for gender equality in Indo-Tibetan Buddhism. For the first time in its history, Bhutan ordained 144 women as nuns, a monumental step initiated by the king himself. This pivotal event not only marks a significant leap forward for Bhutan but also sends a ripple of hope across other nations practicing Indo-Tibetan Buddhism, encouraging them to consider a more inclusive path forward.

The Complex Guru-Disciple Dynamic

When delving into Indo-Tibetan Buddhism and Vajrayāna, one can't help but notice the central role of the guru-disciple relationship. Unlike more straightforward forms of teaching and learning, these traditions elevate the guru-disciple connection to a ritualistic exchange laden with depth and complexity. As a disciple in this setting, you're generally expected to surrender your ego, willingly submit to the guidance and authority of your guru, and delve into practices shrouded in secrecy.

It's within this context of ritual secrecy and spiritual guidance that Vajrayāna distinguishes itself from other Buddhist traditions. This school incorporates tantric elements and secret teachings believed to have been revealed by the Buddha himself. However, this divergence into esoteric practices presents a contrast to what we understand from the Buddha's original teachings. In the EBTs, the Buddha rejects secrecy, advocating for transparency in disseminating his teachings.[58] He encourages his followers to be self-reliant and independent in their understanding of his teachings[59] instead of relying on others.[60] He declares, "I have taught the Dharma without making any distinction between secret and public teachings. The Realized One doesn't have the closed fist of a teacher when it comes to the teachings."[61]

Ethics and Scandals in Vajrayāna Practices

Another significant challenge for Vajrayāna lies in reconciling its key tenets with the dharma. The Buddha teaches that enlightenment is a slow, gradual process,[62] kind of like a craftsperson meticulously refining a piece of silver.[63] He emphasizes that the path to enlightenment comes from gradual training and practice, much like the ocean, which gradually slants, slopes, and inclines, devoid of any abrupt cliffs.[64] He also makes it clear that his own awakening is a product of grit and persistent effort,[65] a step-by-step process that sheds unskillful actions by experiencing their results bit by bit.[66]

Vajrayāna, however, proposes that practitioners can expedite their path to enlightenment through a variety of "skillful means," such as intricate visualization, mantra recitation, mudras, and dedicated rituals like guru yoga, with some advanced practices involving sexual acts. These rituals, which may involve intimate activities with a partner and occasionally the consumption of potent substances, such as sexual fluids and uterine blood, aim not for pleasure but for transformation. They seek to leverage sexual energy to facilitate an awakened mind, leading to a non-dual state of bliss and insight into emptiness. While some practitioners opt for visualization exercises over physical intercourse, others, including former monks, engage in physical acts with their "tantric consorts."

Recent scandals involving exploitation and abuse by teachers from various traditions have cast a shadow over these aspects of Vajrayāna and the wider Buddhist community. Unlike other schools of Buddhism that advocate renunciation of sensuality, Vajrayāna utilizes sexuality as a transformation tool. And, regrettably, this approach has led to misuse due to power dynamics and a lack of clear ethical guidelines, sometimes resulting in instances of abuse and exploitation under the guise of spiritual advancement.

A notable instance is the scandal involving Sogyal Rinpoche, a prominent Tibetan teacher and the founder of the Rigpa spiritual organization. Accused of using his position to maintain a harem of women subjected to various forms of abuse for decades, his case was brought to light in the book *Sex and Violence in Tibetan Buddhism: The Rise and Fall of Sogyal Rinpoche*.

A former member of Rinpoche's inner circle shared her distressing experience: "There must have been about ten women in his inner circle, and it was our job to attend to his every need. We bathed him, dressed him, cooked for him, carried his suitcases, ironed his clothes, and were available for sex. He was a tyrant. Nothing we did was ever good enough. He went into screaming rages and beat us. If I tried to question the way he treated us, he became angry. The only way to avoid this was to stay silent and submissive."

Allegations of sexual misconduct have also been made against Sakyong Mipham Rinpoche, former head of one of the largest Buddhist organizations in the West, and Lama Surya Das, "The American Lama." These incidents are reminders that even in the spiritual sphere—where one might hope to find solace from the shortcomings of human nature—shadows of temptation and weakness persist. Women, unfortunately, often bear the brunt of these transgressions. These cautionary tales also echo the broader concerns about the authenticity of Buddhist texts and practices and the risks when they are shaped by human hands, even those of lamas or monastics.

Rising above Sensual Desires in Buddhist Thought

Buddhism, at its heart, invites us to a journey of liberation—one marked by renunciation, cessation, disenchantment, detachment, contentment, and equanimity. It invites us to step back from the inferno of sensual desires, which, like a moth drawn to light, only serve to snare us in a web of impulsivity and addiction.

In the EBTs, the Buddha declares that a sage remains unstained by sensual pleasures and worldly dust. Their mind rests unsullied like a lotus, its beauty intact despite the muddy waters.[67]

He encourages us to free ourselves from the shackles of discontent and cravings,[68] saying, "When the mind is like a rock, steady, never trembling, free of desire for desirable things, not getting annoyed when things are annoying, from where will suffering strike one whose mind is developed like this?"[69]

The Buddha's teachings are crystal clear—the path to enlightenment involves the cessation of desire and sensuality, not their indulgence.

The Buddha also stresses the importance of evaluating the moral virtue of spiritual teachers.[70] A genuine teacher is reliable, ethical, well-versed in the teachings,[71] and uses the dharma to guide others toward disillusionment with worldly attachments, dispassion for trivial pursuits, and an end to suffering. Such a teacher embodies ethical conduct, patience, love for the teachings, diligence, contentment, mindfulness, and wisdom.[72] They can help uplift our hearts, leading us out of the turmoil of sorrow, lamentation, and distress.[73]

If we can't find such a teacher, the Buddha advises us to turn to the dharma itself, letting its wisdom light our path.[74] He urges us to remain vigilant and self-reliant, understanding that the responsibility of our spiritual growth rests squarely on our own shoulders.[75] After all, the pursuit of enlightenment isn't about conforming to hierarchy or seeking validation from external sources. It's about the inner transformation we experience, the wisdom we cultivate, and the compassion we extend to all beings.

As we close this chapter, I invite you to join me in a quiet reflection, a moment to consider our individual paths within the vast expanse of the dharma. I invite you to look closely at our practices and ask ourselves if they truly resonate with the Buddha's teachings of loving-kindness, ethical conduct, and equanimity. This isn't about finding fault or casting doubt, but rather about ensuring that our spiritual practices are as sincere and constructive as the Buddha intended. Each of us, no matter the tradition we follow, has the opportunity to shine a gentle light on our beliefs, to see if they stand true to the principles that the Buddha lived and taught.

I share these thoughts with you not from a pedestal of perfection but as a fellow traveler on the path. I have not met a flawless teacher or an unblemished tradition; we are all, in our own ways, seeking to better understand and embody the teachings we hold dear. So let's move forward with humility and hope. Our journey toward inner peace and contentment is enriched not by blind adherence but by our brave questioning and our heartfelt striving for truth. Let's embrace this journey together, supporting one another in our shared quest for a practice that not only reflects the wisdom of the dharma but also the truth of our own experiences. Discomfort can lead to growth, and questioning can lead to understanding—this is how we keep the spirit of Buddhism vibrant and alive in our hearts and in the world.

12

Decoding the Divine in the Buddha, Avalokiteśvara, and Amitābha

Let's explore a side of the Buddha that defies our conventional understanding of him. Imagine him as an eternal, infallible celestial being wielding supernatural powers. This divine portrayal can be found in the iconic Chinese epic *Journey to the West.*

Here, we meet the Monkey King, a powerful and mischievous monkey god who creates havoc in the heavenly palace. He not only defeats the Jade Emperor's armies but also loots the palace's orchard of its peaches of immortality. Faced with an unstoppable force, the Jade Emperor turns to the Buddha for help.

In this legendary tale, the Buddha emerges not as a mere spectator or a passive sage but as a dynamic divine force balancing compassion and stern justice. With a simple wave of his hand, he raises a mountain from the ground to imprison the Monkey King, a five-hundred-year lesson in humility.

Fast-forward to Xuanzang, a monk in search of disciples to accompany him on a journey to the West to retrieve sacred

Buddhist sūtras. The reformed Monkey King vows to use his powers to protect Xuanzang from the dangers that lie ahead. Recognizing the Monkey King's potential for good, Xuanzang releases him by removing a magical talisman that the Buddha himself had placed atop the mountain.

While the tales of this fascinating saga are captivating, they bring us to a notable realization. This celestial representation of the Buddha isn't an isolated artistic liberty; it's deeply rooted in Asian arts and literature, with its origins in Mahāyāna Buddhism.

Consider the *Lotus Sūtra*, where the celestial Buddha comes alive, surrounded by an assembly of mythical beings—gods, divas, and dragons. Divine incense fills the air as celestial flowers descend like clouds of floral showers. From the heavens above, thousands of bodhisattvas shower the Buddha with priceless jewels and majestic robes. This Buddha reveals his cosmic lifespan, one that stretches across countless eons. Even though he's still around, he says he chose to pass into *nirvāṇa* in his earthly manifestation as a teaching tool to guide all living beings.

And the mysticism doesn't stop there. In other Mahāyāna texts like the Pure Land *Contemplation Sūtra*, we encounter a dramatic narrative of the Buddha instructing Ānanda to fly "through the sky" to visit a queen, while the Buddha himself teleports to the royal palace.

Meanwhile, in the *Great Nirvāṇa Sūtra*, the Buddha is described as having an eternal, indestructible body whose sustenance doesn't come from earthly food but from spiritual energy. The *King of Concentration Sūtra* takes it up another notch, portraying the Buddha as all-seeing. He knows everything, sees everything, in all the infinite worlds.

These celestial representations, while inspiring, can become stumbling blocks for newcomers, especially those from the West.

They can feel like smoke and mirrors when juxtaposed with the EBTs, where the Buddha's supernatural abilities are mentioned but not emphasized. This distinction is important, as the Buddha himself denies the possibility of any being who "knows all and sees all simultaneously."[1] This stands in line with his teachings on the ever-changing, interdependent nature of existence. The notion of omniscience implies a static, unchanging state of awareness, but the Buddha stresses that our consciousness is not fixed but constantly evolving, shaped by our interactions with the world around us.[2]

And let's not forget the principle of impermanence—one of the Buddha's cornerstone teachings. Everything is in a state of flux. Nothing is eternal. Not even the Buddha himself.

The Buddha's Humanity in Early Texts

In the EBTs, as the Buddha approached his eightieth year, he acknowledged being in the "final stage of life," describing himself as "old, elderly, and advanced in years."[3] His words stirred a wave of sorrow in Ānanda, who worried that he still had much to learn while his beloved teacher was nearing his end. However, the Buddha comforted Ānanda, reminding him that everything born, created, and conditioned must eventually come to an end, including his own body.[4]

Furthermore, the Buddha was no stranger to suffering or pain. During the autumn of his years, he was afflicted with bloody dysentery.[5] Prior to that, his humanity was also echoed in his everyday activities: he took naps,[6] washed his own feet,[7] stretched his back,[8] felt "relaxed when responding to nature's call,"[9] and sought comfort in hot baths during bouts of illness.[10] In his twilight years, his complexion changed. Ānanda even noted how his skin was no longer pure and bright.[11] Such instances serve to illustrate the Buddha as a profoundly human being rather than a divine entity.

Stories of the Buddha and his disciples performing miracles—flying through the air, multiplying themselves, and so forth—appear sporadically in the EBTs. But these should be recognized as later embellishments. Several passages contradict such miraculous accounts, especially those that depict the Buddha as a critic of miracles and psychic wonders. He dismisses them as ignoble and tainted, encouraging instead the cultivation of noble powers such as equanimity, mindfulness, and awareness.[12]

This sentiment is echoed in a narrative where a layman named Kevaddha petitions the Buddha to perform a miracle to kindle faith among the people. The Buddha firmly rejects this idea, telling Kevaddha that the true path to insight is paved with meditation, ethics, knowledge, and wisdom.[13]

In a similar vein, a monk named Sunakkhatta threatens to leave the sangha, disgruntled by the fact that the Buddha does not demonstrate supernatural powers or explain the origin of the world. In response, the Buddha reminds him that such demonstrations and teachings were never part of his mission. His ultimate goal is to guide beings toward the cessation of suffering, and that goal can't be reached through miracles or theories about the world's beginning.[14]

Understanding Enlightenment beyond the Mystical

The EBTs reveal the Buddha's three insights on the brink of his enlightenment: first, remembering his past lives; second, seeing beings passing away and being reborn based on their intentional deeds (karma); and third, understanding the origin, cessation, and path to end suffering. Many Buddhists believe these three insights are essential for achieving enlightenment, so they practice with the goal of having the same realization.

But there are some suttas that hint that the first two insights—remembering past lives and seeing the karmic paths of others—may not be as crucial as people think. A key example is an exchange between the Buddha and a monk named Susīma. Susīma is puzzled because some monks claim enlightenment but lack supernatural abilities like recollecting past lives or seeing people's karmic journeys. "How can you claim you're enlightened when you can't do these things?" Susīma asks.

The monks respond, "We are freed by wisdom."

The Buddha further clarifies to Susīma that enlightenment comes from understanding the reality of the world, not from supernatural abilities.[15]

Other teachings by the Buddha reveal more ways to reach enlightenment, like letting go of cravings,[16] overcoming hindrances, and embracing a noble spectrum of ethics, restraint, mindfulness, and situational awareness.[17] Such practices, grounded in experiential insight, aren't about acquiring mystical or speculative knowledge.

This viewpoint is evident in a dialogue the Buddha has with Venerable Udāyī about the subject of recollection. Udāyī believes that the recollection of past lives is paramount. But the Buddha suggests to Udāyī that he is "not fully committed to the higher mind." He turns to Ānanda and asks how many topics for recollection there were, really.

Ānanda lists five: achieving blissful meditation, gaining knowledge and clarity, giving up sensual desires, uprooting ego, and reaching a higher meditative state by transcending pleasure and pain. To this, the Buddha added a sixth: developing situational awareness and mindfulness in all activities, whether it was walking, eating, or sitting.[18]

This dialogue underscores the Buddha's perspective that remembering past lives isn't as important as the six types of recollections he and Ānanda outline. This view is reiterated in another teaching where the Buddha lists six unsurpassable paths for a devoted practitioner, none of which included remembering past lives or knowing karmic paths. Instead, it's about engaging with the teachings of the Buddha and his disciples through seeing, hearing, acquiring, training, serving, and recollecting. According to the Buddha, the unsurpassable recollection is not about delving into past lives but continuously reflecting on the dharma and applying the teachings to our lives.[19]

When we consider the first two pieces of knowledge that supposedly emerge at the brink of the Buddha's enlightenment, their relevance comes into question. After all, with spiritual goals like understanding suffering;[20] abandoning desire;[21] ending defilements;[22] eliminating greed, hate, and delusion;[23] and attaining peace and awakening in this life,[24] how are these objectives connected to recalling past lives or having a karmic vision? Wouldn't it make more sense to focus on the tangible, the experiential, the here and now?

In several teachings, the Buddha encourages us to let go of dwelling on the past and yearning for the future, urging us instead to anchor ourselves in the present moment. This idea is articulated in the following verse:

> Don't run back to the past,
> don't hope for the future.

What's past is left behind;
the future has not arrived;
and phenomena in the present
are clearly seen in every case.
Knowing this, foster it—
unfaltering, unshakable.[25]

This emphasis on the present suggests a practice focused on the now—on the actionable, the tangle, and the immediate experiences that shape our spiritual journey. This focus on the present underlines a recurring theme in Buddhist texts that while supernatural narratives can fascinate, they should not distract us from the Buddha's essential teachings: to lessen suffering and cultivate clarity, contentment, and equanimity in our immediate journey.

Avalokiteśvara's Many Forms

In Mahāyāna Buddhism, we encounter divine beings like Avalokiteśvara and Amitābha. These celestial figures, who assist us in everything from conceiving a son to entering paradise, also make us wonder how they fit into the bigger picture of Buddhism.

Let's start with Avalokiteśvara. As depicted in the *Lotus Sūtra*, he's a master of disguise. He morphs into countless forms to help those in need. One moment, he's an immortal general. The next, a pure maiden. And at times, even a dragon to help other . . . dragons. Each transformation comes with the tools needed to help people—and dragons. Artists often depict this by giving him multiple arms, each one holding a unique tool for his rescue missions.

In the captivating world of Chinese historical dramas—a realm you've probably guessed by now that I enthusiastically frequent—Guānyīn, the Chinese manifestation of Avalokiteśvara, often graces the screen as a deity who blessed families with fertility and sons. In the popular 2018 series *Story of Yanxi Palace*, there's an intriguing scene where a daring noble consort gifts the empress a golden Guānyīn statue. The statue is a birthday gift, but it's a backhanded one. It's a subtle nudge, reminding the empress that she needs divine intervention to bear a male heir.

When the empress sees the statue, she freezes. Her eyes narrow to slits, the tension palpable in the air, and her lips pinch into a thin, rigid line. A moment later, they curve into a tight, strained smile, the epitome of forced graciousness. As a queen expected to uphold her grace and dignity at all times, there's little she can do but accept the gift, her silent indignation masked by a veneer of royal composure.

This scene is a perfect example of how Chinese historical dramas can be both entertaining and thought-provoking. The enduring popularity of Guānyīn is a testament to how these elements of Buddhist mythology have seamlessly interwoven with local customs and beliefs over the centuries.

The Forty-Eight Vows of Dharmākara

The Pure Land School of Buddhism also holds Avalokiteśvara in high esteem. This school sees him as the earthly manifestation of Amitābha, a deity revered in several East Asian countries, including China, Việt Nam, Japan, and South Korea.

The *Infinite Life Sūtra* serves as a key text in understanding the foundation of this school. It tells us that Amitābha was once a humble monk known as Dharmākara. Dharmākara makes a series of forty-eight vows, each designed to assist any being who seeks his help. His goal was to enable them to be reborn in the Pure Land, the Land of Bliss, and ultimately attain enlightenment.

The vows Dharmākara makes are not only ambitious but also quite extraordinary. He speaks of a Pure Land where beings would live forever, communicate telepathically, and bask in endless peace and happiness. Inhabitants would also embody the thirty-two marks of a great man. Women—if they wish—would have the chance to transcend their female form to be reborn in the Land of Bliss.

Dharmākara is so committed to these vows that he declares he won't attain buddhahood unless all of them are fulfilled. And since he is now known as Amitābha, it implies that his vows have indeed been realized.

Yes. Every single one of them. Including the one about the thirty-two marks of a great man, which are mentioned not only in this sūtra but also in several other Buddhist texts.[26]

What are some of these marks? They include golden skin, deep blue eyes, muscles bulging in seven places, a jaw like a lion, calves like an antelope, and a head shaped like a turban. The list goes on with forty teeth, a foreskin encasing the penis, skin so delicate it repels dust and dirt, and a body proportionate to a banyan tree, with an arm span equal to the height. One even speaks of the palms' ability to touch the knees while standing upright without bending—ring any bells?

These are an array of unusual features, aren't they? Apparently, some of them have roots in the hymns of the Hindu tradition.[27] So it's puzzling how Buddhism, with its fundamentally different teachings, decided to adopt these physical attributes.

It's even more head-scratching considering that if the Buddha himself possessed these traits, he would look very different from everyone else. But he seemed like an everyday Joe, as detailed in other parts of the EBTs. A layman named Pukkusāti didn't recognize him,[28] and King Ajātasattu mistook him for an ordinary monk.[29]

Moreover, some of these marks defy the laws of biology. Humans usually have thirty-two teeth, not forty. No skin, no matter how delicate, can repel dust and dirt. Having an arm span equal to the height might be typical, but for the palms to touch the knees while standing upright without bending is a physical impossibility. As for the blue eyes and golden skin, they probably reflect the societal norms of ancient India, where these traits are seen as signs of prestige and power.

Before his enlightenment, the Buddha practiced extreme asceticism, pushing his body so far that his spine protruded through his stomach. Even after adopting the middle way and resuming eating, he usually had one meal a day, which likely kept him pretty lean. So how did he manage to get muscles bulging in seven places?

The Buddha's Definition of a "Great Man"

Some scholars think these marks were included to earn brownie points with the Hindu community—an odd choice, given that the Buddha teaches that a person's worth isn't tied to their physical attributes. He says that not nobility, physical beauty, nor wealth made someone better or worse.[30]

In one conversation, when Sāriputta asks how a "great man" is defined, the Buddha replies, "A great man is one whose mind is free."[31] He expands on this in other teachings, defining a great man as someone who lives spiritually among worldly desires, rises above craving, and maintains mindfulness. Such a person achieves peace and is free from all disturbances.[32]

Furthermore, the Buddha explicitly advises against getting caught up in things like palmistry, protective chanting, or divination from bodily marks.[33] He maintains that those walking the path of righteousness should abandon all superstitions tied to bodily marks.[34]

Rituals and the Illusion of Divine Power

At the heart of Pure Land Buddhism lies Dharmākara's eighteenth vow. This vow asserts that anyone who sincerely entrusts themselves to Amitābha, wishes to be reborn in the Pure Land, and invokes his name—even just ten times—will be rewarded a rebirth in the Pure Land. Accordingly, the main practice of this school involves chanting Amitābha's name and the Pure Land sūtras.

As discussed earlier, this reliance on divine intervention contradicts the principles of self-reliance and moral responsibility emphasized in the EBTs. The Buddha teaches that we must be our own refuge and do the necessary work ourselves.[35] His teachings serve merely as a guide.[36] They light our path, but it's up to us to tread the journey through our own understanding rather than depending on external sources.[37] In fact, the Buddha openly refutes the concept of a savior deity, stating that "the world has no shelter or savior."[38]

For those who attribute all events to a divine creator, the Buddha says that such an approach is tantamount to submitting our moral compass to the unpredictable rise and fall of the tides. He challenges these individuals, stating, "There are some ascetics who believe everything experienced—pleasurable, painful, or neutral—is the result of a divine creator's work. To them I say, 'In that case, you might justify harming living beings, stealing, lying, sowing discord, or harboring harmful thoughts—all under the banner of divine creation.' Those who place divine creation above all else lack motivation, effort, and the discernment between right and wrong. Their lack of mindfulness and vigilance prevent them from being true ascetics."[39]

Once, a Brahmin teacher named Bhāradvāja asked the Buddha if he meditated in the wilderness to be in the company of the thirty-three gods in heaven. The Buddha declined, saying he had let go of all his hopes and desires, even those tied to the afterlife. With the snare of ignorance discarded, he was unshackled, free to meditate with a vision as clear as a mountain spring. In this state, he was at peace with himself and his desires.[40]

This sentiment—the Buddha's call for liberation from the longing for rebirth in other realms[41]—echoes throughout the EBTs. He compares such yearnings to heavy chains that bind the heart, hinder spiritual progress, and distract the mind from true commitment, effort, and perseverance.[42] He teaches that a person who has achieved serenity and detachment wouldn't yearn for rebirth or chase after worldly desires.[43]

The Buddha also speaks to the impermanence of material possessions. He notes that the shine of a palace, cast on the northern quarter, is fleeting. A wise person, recognizing the impermanence and the constant change in the material world, would not find lasting pleasure in it.[45]

During the Buddha's time, Hinduism's elaborate ceremonies and devotions dominated the spiritual landscape. But the

Buddha pointed out that these rituals were often pursued for pleasure and material gain. He teaches that genuine peace and liberation from suffering come from cultivating the mind, not from the hollow recitation of prayers or the reliance on external forces.[46]

When a follower asked whether the rituals advocated by the Western Brahmins could lead a person to heaven, the Buddha said:

> "What do you think? Take a person who kills living creatures, steals, commits sexual misconduct. They use speech that's false, divisive, harsh, or nonsensical. They're greedy, malicious, and harbor wrong views. And a large crowd comes together, offering prayers and praise, circumambulating them with joined palms, wishing for their rebirth in a good place, a heavenly realm. Do you think that person would be reborn in heaven because of these prayers?"

"No, sir," the follower responded.[47]

The Buddha urges us to let go of vices such as prayer, deception, greed, and indulgence, encouraging us instead to embrace a life of virtue.[48] He makes it clear: repeating sacred texts isn't enough.[49] We can chant mantras all day long, but that won't rectify a life mired in dishonesty and corruption.[50] It's like trying to wash a dirty shirt by singing to it.

I understand the appeal of having figures like Avalokiteśvara and Amitābha in our spiritual landscapes. Many of us think of them as a warm, cozy blanket on a cold, stormy night. When life feels like an unending downpour, these divine beings offer a refuge, a tender haven for hearts heavy with the burdens of the world. Mahāyāna Buddhism is a school that aspires to ferry every single person to the shores of liberation. The inclusion of these celestial figures serves as a beacon for those who, due to the constraints of time or circumstances, find themselves unable to immerse fully in the depths of spiritual practice.

But let's not mistake the blanket for the fireplace. The real warmth of Buddhism doesn't come from some promised celestial comfort. It's about transforming our lives, right here, right now, through turning our blind spots into moments of clarity, the bitterness of hate into the warmth of love, and our fears into audacious courage. It's about engaging wholeheartedly in the present, embracing our lives as they unfold, and drawing strength and wisdom from the experiences we encounter day by day. This path is about understanding the nature of suffering, recognizing the deep connections we share with all beings, and striving to lead a life filled with meaning and purpose, even when times are tough. By resolving to harness the full potential of our present reality, instead of getting swept away by the promises of distant realms or future rewards, we turn every challenge into an opportunity to deepen our understanding, compassion, and connection with the world around us.

13

Prātimokṣha and Monastic Constraints

Cast your mind back to chapter 5 and our journey through the metaphor of arrows—each one symbolizing an obstacle, a hurdle, a source of pain that has made navigating the spiritual landscape of Buddhism challenging for women. As we transition our focus from the broader aspects of Buddhist practices to a closer look at monastic life, we're about to confront another sharp arrow. This one is not just casually lying on the spiritual path but is deeply entrenched in the monastic system itself.

The prātimokṣha, or monastic code, is a set of guidelines that outlines the conduct of Buddhist monks and nuns. On the surface, it seems like a well-intentioned compass directing monastics toward an environment ripe for spiritual growth. But scratch beneath that surface and we find a more complex picture. Just like any other social construct, the prātimokṣha is vulnerable to the biases and limitations of the time and culture in which it was formed.

Within this context, I've found that Buddhists—consciously or unconsciously—tend to downplay the glaring disparities between the rules imposed on nuns versus monks. Some point to differences in biology and behavior, while others portray these extra rules for nuns as a "safety net." According to this line of thought, women, being more "vulnerable," benefit from these added restrictions as a form of protection. While this narrative may offer a comforting tale that seemingly absolves the monastic order of any discriminatory practices, it simultaneously perpetuates a hidden form of gender bias. This outlook doesn't just pat monks on the back; it places an undue burden on nuns, singling them out for their so-called vulnerability. What's often overlooked are the real-world implications that these outdated, unnecessary, and, frankly, sexist rules have on a nun's spiritual and psychological well-being.

Take a trip with me back to 2017. You may recall from earlier chapters that I was at a Vietnamese Zen monastery in El Paso, contemplating nunhood. A seasoned nun there advised me to stay a layperson to maintain my "freshness and carefreeness." She highlighted that the commitment to 348 precepts, along with countless other cultural, societal, and communal norms, could transform me into someone "stern and rigid." She said, "As a lay practitioner, you can still serve the sangha through acts of service without the crushing weight of monastic life."

A monk expressed similar sentiments, suggesting that taking on nunhood might chip away at my natural cheerfulness. He noted that without skillful navigation, I could become "dry and joyless." Now, it's worth mentioning that his viewpoint was not entirely altruistic. At the time, he was contemplating an exit from monastic life and was actively encouraging me to leave the monastery with him. Nevertheless, their cautionary tales start to resonate as we delve deeper into the prātimokṣha.

First, given this common thread in their advice, we're prompted to ask: Why are nuns burdened with this web of rules when the Buddha never explicitly crafted the Vinaya Piṭaka, the complex set of monastic laws that includes the prātimokṣha? Tradition claims the Buddha laid down these rules, yet historical scrutiny reveals that most Vinaya texts were codified between the first and fifth centuries CE—nearly a thousand years after the Buddha's passing. Could it be that these rules aren't the Buddha's teachings but rather a fusion of centuries-old cultural and societal norms cemented into religious law?

Take a look at the three surviving Vinaya traditions: the Dharmaguptaka, practiced in East Asia, has 250 rules for monks and 348 for nuns; the Theravāda, practiced in South and Southeast Asia, has 227 rules for monks and 311 for nuns; and the Mūlasarvāstivāda, practiced in Tibet and Mongolia, has 253 rules for monks and 364 rules for nuns. Putting the obvious disparity aside, can we picture the Buddha—the Liberated One, the Fearless One, the Ultimate Radical—living by these two-hundred-plus monastic rules to guide his every action? Would he have endorsed this way of life?

Let's delve into the Theravāda pātimokkha (the Pāli equivalent of the Sanskrit prātimokṣha) and examine some of its rules relating to women and nuns:

- Not to lie down in a building where a woman is present
- Not to teach a woman more than six consecutive words of dharma
- Not to teach nuns without obtaining permission from the sangha

* Not to proceed to a nuns' monastery for teaching
* Not to eat food prepared by a nun
* Not to accept food from a nun
* To dismiss the nuns who manage the service to the monks to go somewhere else during the meal

Then there are these five rules about carpets alone:

* Not to accept carpets containing silk
* Not to accept floor carpets only made of black sheep wool
* Not to accept a floor carpet that is more than half made with black sheep wool and a quarter with white wool
* Not to make a new carpet without adding a part of the old one
* Not to purchase another floor carpet if the former is not yet six years old

Let's state the obvious here: Buddhism is the path of liberation, not the path of carpet management. The EBTs contain no rules from the Buddha concerning carpets. It doesn't take a rocket scientist to see that most of these rules don't reflect the Buddha's signature voice of reason and practicality. Can we picture the Buddha, beneath his bodhi tree, lecturing about carpets?

"Mendicants," he begins, with an air of gravity, "we must speak about carpets."

A murmur ripples through his disciples—earnest mendicants, sitting cross-legged, who, moments ago, were ready to grasp the wisdom of the ages. *Carpets? Did he say carpets?*

"Yes, carpets," the Buddha continues. "Replacing them after five years is premature. Seven years is utterly negligent. But six years . . . ah, six is the Middle Path of carpet longevity. Commit this to memory for the welfare, benefit, and happiness of all beings."

Of course, this never happened. But it's amusing to think that the rules of pātimokkha have become so hyperspecific that they address these sorts of details. And it raises the question: Are these rules truly a reflection of Buddhist principles, or are they the work of control-loving editors exerting authority over every facet of monastic life, no matter how trivial?

Fast-forward to today, and some monastics adhere religiously to these rules, while others, even if not strictly compliant, refrain from criticizing them. Why is that? Well, there's a rule for that too. Confessional rule number seventy-two prohibits monastics from disparaging the rules of the pātimokkha.

This rule also exists in the Dharmaguptaka prātimokṣha of the Mahāyāna school. The 2003 revised version by Plum Village states, "A monastic who complains about the precepts and fine manners, saying that the articles presented are bothersome, too complicated, too detailed, not truly necessary, or that they take away one's freedom, commits an Expression of Regret Offense."

So even if the rules are indeed bothersome, complex, overly detailed, unnecessary, and sexist, this built-in fear of speaking up hinders real change. It's like living under a regime where the media can't critique the government—praises and positive spin only.

In 2003, when Thích Nhất Hạnh unveiled the revised prātimokṣha, the reaction was mixed. The Dharma Teacher Council of Plum Village spent five years crafting this updated prātimokṣha, consulting with Vinaya teachers, monks, and nuns from Việt Nam and beyond. They aimed to update the prātimokṣha, enhancing its relevance and adaptability to the realities and cultural dynamics of current times. However, some

Buddhists perceived it as a deviation from the established Vinaya tradition, arguing that the changes diverged from the Buddha's original teachings. They would have preferred a grand council of all Buddhists to deliberate collectively on any changes rather than a single group making unilateral decisions. Yet in today's world, with its medley of schools and traditions, such a task seemed unfeasible. Perhaps acknowledging this, Thích Nhất Hạnh boldly declared that "the Buddha needs courageous disciples to make this revolutionary step."

Thích Nhất Hạnh was well aware that his initiative would cause a stir in the Buddhist world, but he charged ahead anyway. To an outsider, it might appear somewhat radical. However, a look into Buddhism's history reveals this is how these rulebooks have developed over the centuries. There is no single, unified Vinaya or prātimokṣha. The number of rules varies from tradition to tradition, shaped by different social and cultural contexts. Out of 18 schools, all of them varied in the number of precepts, with some schools having as few as 195 precepts and others having as many as 364 precepts. The content of the precepts also differs from tradition to tradition. Some precepts are found in all schools, while others are unique to one or two schools.

Additionally, it's widely known that monastics rarely follow all the stipulations of their chosen Vinaya lineage in practice. For instance, although all schools' prātimokṣha rules prohibit the use of money, it's nevertheless utilized by the vast majority of monastics. This raises a question: What's the point of a rulebook if the monastics don't follow all the rules? Clearly, it's not due to a lack of effort. It's simply impossible in this day and age to avoid dealing with money. The prudent course of action, thus, is to modify the rulebook to reflect modern needs and norms while ensuring that it still aligns with the spirit of Buddhism.

While I was among those who applauded Thích Nhất Hạnh's effort, in my humble opinion, the tweaks to the 2003 Dharmaguptaka prātimokṣha weren't "revolutionary" enough. It's like upgrading an old jailhouse with a fresh coat of paint, new flooring, snazzy furniture, and updated security and programs. It looks better, feels better, but it's still a jailhouse. The difference in the number of offenses and the disparity between the precepts for monks and nuns remain startling. Monks have four rules that result in immediate expulsion. But nuns? They have twice as many. The inequality continues across various categories of rules: monks must adhere to 27 Sangha Restoration Offenses and nuns to 36. Monks have 32 Release and Expression of Regret Offenses, and nuns bear the burden of 40. Ultimately, monks are guided by 250 rules, while nuns must navigate 348.

When we delve into the rules themselves, we see an uneven punishment for crossing the line. Both monks and nuns risk expulsion for committing any of the "big four" degradation offenses—sexual intercourse, theft, murder, or false claims of spiritual enlightenment.

Yet, when it comes to four additional degradation offenses tied to sexual conduct—offenses include engaging in or allowing sexually motivated touching (Degradation Offenses 5 and 6), sparking sexual desire in someone (Degradation Offense 7), or consenting to sexual relations (Degradation Offense 8)—any of these offenses can lead to a nun's expulsion.

But what about the monks? If they commit offenses 5 and 7, they're merely put on the bench for a while—spending some time "dwelling apart" from the sangha and making amends before a Ceremony of Purification. Meanwhile, offenses 6 and 8 are absent from the monks' prātimokṣha, revealing a blatant disparity in how each gender is held accountable.

This uneven field extends beyond sexual conduct. Some rules, like refraining from overeating (Expression of Regret Offense 97) or from throwing someone's belongings in anger (Expression of Regret Offense 42), are mysteriously absent from the monks' prātimokṣha. Why are these rules only applicable to nuns and not monks? Aren't men just as prone to grabbing that second helping of dessert or lashing out in anger?

Upon further examination, we find that nuns are subject to seventy-one additional precepts compared to monks, often because single monk precepts are divided into multiple ones for nuns. This not only simplifies transgression for nuns but also reveals that sixty-one of these additional precepts—with only ten reflecting biological differences—are applicable to both genders.

In 2005, after nearly four decades of exile, Thích Nhất Hạnh set foot in his homeland of Việt Nam. Greeted by cheering crowds, he made a remarkable gesture during a Lunar New Year event in Huế City. To the awe of onlookers, he prostrated himself—not once, not twice, but three times—before a group of nuns seated with their palms joined. This simple act was like a burst of sunlight piercing the clouds. The senior monks of Vietnamese nationality standing beside him were somewhat taken aback, but they followed suit nonetheless.

While the idea of showing such respect to nuns might have been somewhat foreign to these monks, it's an ordinary occurrence in Thích Nhất Hạnh's Western monasteries. Going a step further, Thích Nhất Hạnh even allowed nuns to reordain his tradition against the guidance of the Dharmaguptaka Vinaya, which permits monks to reordain a total of seven times, but a nun cannot reordain under any circumstance.

Daoxuan, the Chinese patriarch of the Vinaya school, whose Dharmagupta commentaries have become standard guidelines, expressed the following sentiment in the sixth-century *Commentary on the Bhikṣuṇīs of the Dharmaguptaka Vinaya*: "The mind of women is weak, and they are not capable of promoting the Buddhist path. They were not allowed [to enter the monastic order] in the first place, so how could it be acceptable suddenly to allow them to be re-ordained?"

Thích Nhất Hạnh, with his compassionate and courageous heart, has done his part to challenge this antiquated and ignorant view. Now it's our turn to step up to the plate. And our journey begins with us recognizing and confronting these old-fashioned, prejudiced views for what they are—sexism. Any institution that not only gives women fewer rights and opportunities but also burdens them with more restrictive rules is fundamentally sexist. This double standard—less freedom and more obligations—magnifies the urgency for change.

As Buddhists, we must question why our religion carries this sexist label, especially when the Buddha is known as the first emancipator of women, the first spiritual leader who gave equal opportunities to everyone regardless of their creed, race, social status, and gender.

It's widely accepted among contemporary scholars that the monastic rules have been subject to significant human interference. Yet many of us still regard these rules as the sacred truth.

Within the EBTs, we find a single instance where the monastic code is articulated. Its simplicity and focus on moral and ethical conduct stands in stark contrast to the elaborate human additions. This sutta states:

> Patient acceptance is the ultimate austerity.
> Extinguishment is the ultimate
> No true renunciate injures another,
> nor does an ascetic hurt another.

> Not to do any evil;
> to embrace the good;
> to purify one's mind:
> this is the instruction of the buddhas.
> Not speaking ill nor doing harm;
> restraint in the monastic code;
> moderation in eating;
> staying in remote lodgings;
> commitment to the higher mind—
> this is the instruction of the buddhas.[1]

This code, stripped to its essence, is transparent and manageable. It doesn't delve into intricate details but rather champions overarching principles like patience, acceptance, moral integrity, and wisdom. While structure is needed in communal life, an excess of petty restrictions breeds mistrust and limits freedom—contradicting the heart of Buddhist practice.

As seekers, we must examine where these elaborations stray from the Buddha's intentions. Rules shaped by cultural biases cannot equitably guide the sangha. Only by balancing wisdom and compassion can we craft a monastic ethic that allows individuals to flourish, united in our shared humanity.

The journey forward calls for open hearts and open minds—a willingness to see the best in one another. Let the profound wisdom of the dharma be our guiding light, and not be swayed by the forces of fear, bias, or desire for control. Let us sculpt the monastic code in a way that honors the dharma's highest aspiration—liberation. Let us strive for a spiritual sanctuary that fosters freedom, empowerment, and personal growth. Our reimagined monastic life should serve a vivid testament to trust, mutual respect, shared responsibility, and a peaceful harmony that brings the dharma into full bloom.

14

Questioning the Gatekeepers of Buddhism

The ongoing search for wisdom demands that we continually challenge and reassess our long-held beliefs and assumptions. In previous chapters, we have explored the misconception that women are in some way spiritually inferior, a belief perpetuated by certain monks and ancient texts. These arrows of misunderstandings are not rooted in the Buddha's original teachings but rather evolved over time, layered with cultural and patriarchal biases. Now, let's explore two more arrows embedded in some Buddhist traditions: the belief that being born female is a result of past bad karma and the notion that Buddhist scriptures are intended primarily for monks, essentially making them the exclusive heirs and keepers of the Buddha's legacy.

The notion that one's gender is a reflection of past-life karma isn't rooted in the EBTs but in the later Pāli commentaries and various Mahāyāna sūtras. These late texts present a patriarchal view of society where women are depicted as beings with limited agency.

One key figure contributing to this narrative is Buddhaghosa, a prominent Theravāda commentator of the Sutta Nipāta. He sketches women as fickle, greedy, easily seduced, and prone to infidelity given the right conditions. He asserts that women should obey their husbands and frames them as unpredictable creatures whose minds are hard to understand. He spins a tale in his *Dhammapada* Verse 43 commentary about Soreyya, a wealthy man's son. When Soreyya encounters the golden-skinned monk Thera Mahākaccāyana, he wishes his wife shared the same complexion. Even more bizarrely, he fantasizes about the monk himself being his wife. This fleeting thought triggers an immediate transformation into a woman.

In her new identity, Soreyya flees in shame to Taxila. There, she marries a wealthy man, gives birth to two children, and lives a life far removed from her previous existence. When an old friend recognizes her, she confesses her story, revealing the consequences of her misguided desire toward Thera Mahākaccāyana. To correct her "mistake," she seeks the monk's forgiveness, which he grants, and she instantly reverts to her male form. Now back as a man, Soreyya chooses the path of renunciation, joining the sangha, and ultimately attains arahantship.

This story essentially suggests a sort of "punishment" in Soreyya's transformation into a woman and a "reward" in his return to male form, subtly implying a hierarchy between male and female experiences. Moreover, despite being a parent in both forms, Soreyya expresses a deeper affection for the children born while he was a woman, only to renounce this affection after reaching arahantship. This story hints at a dichotomy: the emotional nature of femininity and the enlightened detachment of masculinity.

In the Pāli Canon, we also find instances like the narrative of Gopikā, suggesting a transition from female to male as a move toward a higher state of existence.[1] This account, along with similar tales in later scriptures such as the Mahāyāna *Great Compassion Dharani Sūtra*—where Avalokiteśvara promises that if a woman wishing to become a man recites a particular chant but fails to change from female to male, Avalokiteśvara won't achieve enlightenment.

These are mere glimpses into the many texts perpetuating the idea that women's birth is a lesser state, a karmic consequence of past wrongs, while men have seemingly hit the karmic jackpot.

However, such stories contradict the Buddha's consistent message in the EBTs that human birth itself—regardless of gender—is a rare and precious opportunity, the result of good karma.[2] He stresses the invaluable nature of human life,[3] highlighting our incredible opportunity to grow and evolve spiritually.[4]

In Buddhism, karma is not determined by biological attributes but by ethical considerations rooted in the mind and consciousness. Our actions and intentions are the paintbrushes that color our present life and the ones that follow.[5] As the Buddha teaches, "Bad destinies of whatever kind, in this world or the next, are all rooted in ignorance, compounded of greed and desire."[6] Thus, it is through dispelling ignorance and fostering skillful qualities that we shape our destiny, not through the arbitrary conditions of our birth.

Expanding on this idea, the Buddha offers four consolations in this life if our minds are free of hatred and ill will, uncorrupted and purified:

1. If there's a life after this one, and good and bad deeds have a result, we'll be reborn in a good place.
2. If this life is all there is, and our actions have no cosmic consequences, we still get to live this life happily, unburdened by hate.

3. If bad things happen to people who do bad things, then we, with our clear conscience, can sidestep that misery.
4. If bad things don't happen to people who do bad things, then we can still look in the mirror and see a person pure and untainted by wrongdoing.[7]

As you can see, the Buddha's teachings focus on ethical conduct. A life of "unprincipled and immoral conduct" might land us in a less than desirable place after death. But a life of principled and moral conduct could lead to rebirth in a good place.[8]

Did the Buddha ever single out women as carriers of bad karma in these teachings? No. Yet this misconception has taken root, thanks to certain monks pushing their patriarchal views. As a result, some female practitioners have internalized this perceived inferiority, striving to accumulate as much merit as they can, all in the hope of being reborn as a man.

With all due respect, those who twisted the Buddha's teachings on karma for their own gain can be seen as exhibiting "unprincipled and immoral conduct." So if it turns out "there's life after this one, and good and bad deeds have a result," let us keep them in our thoughts and prayers.

As we've explored in previous chapters, life's hardships aren't a product of karma. There's a bigger picture, where cultural, historical, and social forces interplay. For women, it often feels like the game was rigged from the start. We're wrestling with antiquated prejudices, society's "how-to-be-a-woman" handbook, and institutions that seem to enjoy a complex chess game, setting us up against challenges and then pointing fingers at us for our position on the board.

And what about the texts where the Buddha seems to speak exclusively to monks? Or, as seen in some Mahāyāna sūtras, "sons"? Well, considering that the authors of these texts were monks themselves, it's not surprising that their primary audience would be men. But imagine if they had allowed nuns and laypeople to participate in the recitation councils—these texts might have been far more inclusive and balanced.

Scholars like Dr. Alice Collett and Venerable Bhikkhu Anālayo offer a fresh lens to view this issue. They suggest that words such as *bhikkhave* and *bhikkhu* were used as umbrella terms covering monks, nuns, and sometimes laypeople. These terms were used in a generic sense, not specifically gendered. Also, when the Buddha referred to multiple monks, he would use *Sariputtas* instead of *Sariputta*—a reflection of Sāriputta's position as the Buddha's chief disciple. Therefore, when the Buddha says *monks*, he's addressing everyone present, not just the male monastics.

Bhante Sujato embraces this inclusive interpretation in his translations of the Sutta Piṭaka, opting for *they/them* and *mendicants* to replace the traditional gendered terms. Now, that's what we call progress—a step toward true inclusivity and equality.

Flowing toward a Dynamic Future

As we approach the close of this chapter, let's turn our attention to Dr. Joongpyo Lee, a former Korean monk. Dr. Lee courageously stepped back to reexamine his Mahāyāna monastic training through the lens of the earliest Buddhist teachings. This intellectual journey led him to translate the Pāli Canon into modern Korean and establish Buddhanara, an organization devoted to spreading wisdom, equality, and peace.

Dr. Lee's journey showcases the power of reflection and self-inquiry in enriching our spiritual lives. Just as he found his way back to the Buddha's original teachings, we all possess the ability to reset our spiritual compass when we feel adrift. His message is clear: The essence of Buddhism can only be found when we peel back the layers of external influences and rediscover its elemental principles.

Reflecting on the many ideas, assumptions, and viewpoints in this book, I realize that some may challenge your perspectives or cause discomfort. However, I urge you to consider that discomfort as an invitation to reassess, to let down your defenses, and to welcome the unknown with curiosity.

I must admit that for a long time, I, too, have felt a little lost. Like someone wandering in a forest without a compass, walking in endless circles. Since reigniting my interest in Buddhism, I've explored numerous Buddhist traditions without finding one that feels completely like home. Despite earnest attempts to live by Buddhist teachings, societal norms and pressures sometimes sway me off my path. Yet setbacks and detours shouldn't define our journey—neither yours nor mine.

The Buddha teaches that existence is like a river in constant flux. Our beliefs and understanding should reflect this natural flow. Anchoring ourselves to one viewpoint limits our spiritual growth, which should come from active questioning rather than passive acceptance. We must scrutinize not just the ancient texts but also the institutions that protect them. Change is already happening, and it's not limited to academics and translators. Women are increasingly gaining ordination and stepping into leadership roles. Monastic orders are growing more inclusive of LGBTQIA+ individuals. Tech-savvy younger generations are employing social media to broadcast a more accessible and varied image of modern-day Buddhism. Some are even reinterpreting traditional teachings through the social justice lens, ensuring that Buddhism remains a relevant force for positive change in the world.

If Dr. Joongpyo Lee could critically assess and modify his own traditions, so can we. Like the Buddha, we must muster the courage to defy norms that no longer serve us.

So let's engage in dialogues, expand our horizons, dig deeper into both well-known and obscure texts, and, above all, apply this inquisitive spirit in our daily practice. Every day is a new curve in the ever-changing river of dharma, guiding us toward deeper understanding, greater inclusivity, and boundless compassion.

As we forge ahead on our quest for intellectual and spiritual growth, let these timeless words from the *Dhammapada* be our guide:

> Better to live a single day
> seeing the supreme teaching
> than to live a hundred years
> blind to the supreme teaching.
>
> Better than reciting
> a hundred meaningless verses
> is a single saying of Dharma,
> hearing which brings you peace.[9]

15

A Glimpse into the Buddha's Personality

As we open the last chapter of our shared journey, let's take a moment to reflect on the stories, teachings, and reflections that have brought us to this point. It's a fitting time to return to the Buddha's narratives—stories that were embedded in my early life as the joy of sun-soaked barbecues are for many American children. Some of these tales have stuck with me like chewed gum to the underside of a school desk.

Let's start with the Jātaka tale of King Shibi. Once upon a time, he was the Buddha in a past life. One fateful day, a terrified little dove dove (pun intended) into his royal court, seeking refuge from a hungry hawk. The king found himself torn, moved by the dove's desperate fight for life and yet aware of the hawk's natural need to hunt. So the king made a remarkable proposition: a chunk of his own flesh, equal in weight to the dove. The hawk was taken aback by the king's offer, but it agreed. And so the king cut off a piece of himself, feeding the hawk and sparing the dove.

As a youngster, this tale stirred something deep within me. The Buddha's readiness to sacrifice his own flesh put my whining over scraped knees into stark perspective. Furthermore, my Vietnamese name, Yến Nhi, translates to "a little canary," which created a personal connection—at least in my mind—between the dove and the Buddha's act of compassion and myself.

However, as I grew older, I came to understand that these tales were not meant to be taken at face value. Instead, they were symbolic vessels, crafted to convey lessons of compassion and empathy. But with this newfound understanding also came confusion and a feeling of betrayal. I was left questioning whether the real, historical Buddha would be as compassionate as King Shibi. And was it indeed wise or, as some would argue, recklessly altruistic to sacrifice one's flesh to save a bird? Should we intervene in such situations, or should we step aside, letting nature's survival-of-the-fittest rule take its course? Life, much like a chessboard, often demands thoughtful deliberation on where our efforts will make the most impact. And frankly, the idea of donating human flesh to wildlife seems like a questionable allocation of resources.

So this Jātaka tale, designed to inspire, left me wrestling with more questions than answers.

Fast-forward a few years, and I discovered that the Buddha had a preference for sleeping on his right side, a position referred to as the lion's posture. This position relieves pressure on the heart by expanding space in the chest cavity. That seemed logical enough to me. So, like a kid copying a celebrity's haircut, I embraced it.

I slept like that for years. Right side, every night, convinced it was the wise thing to do. However, over time, I noticed a peculiar change. My face appeared slightly off-balance. The right side was puffier, the jaw more pronounced. I could see it clearly in photos. My Sherlock senses surmised it had to do with my sleep position. Was my pursuit of imitating the Buddha backfiring?

Undeterred, I decided to flip the script. Switch from right to left. Not an easy task, mind you. Two decades of a habit doesn't change overnight. But I was determined. Didn't want a lopsided face.

Two years later, and things are looking up. My face is on the mend. Slowly but surely, symmetry is making a comeback. Not quite there yet, but progress is in sight.

So what wisdom can we glean from these experiences? As we go through life, our understanding of tales and teachings, such as those of the Buddha, evolves. They can inspire, confuse, or prompt us to make changes in our own lives. As we mature, we begin to see the depth and nuance in these narratives, which, in turn, shape our viewpoints, actions, and choices. However, it's important to remember that it's perfectly fine to learn from our missteps, adjust our trajectory, and keep moving forward. The trick is to tackle everything with discernment, a dash of practicality, and a spoonful of common sense. Sometimes we need to do what's best for us, even if it means not always following the Buddha's footsteps as depicted in tales and scriptures.

As we delve into the EBTs in the following pages, we'll catch intimate glimpses of the Buddha's inner universe. We'll observe his preference for silence and solitude, the mindful equilibrium in every aspect of his life, and the compassion evident in his words and actions. I've stumbled, tripped, and dusted myself off so you don't have to. But remember, a pinch of salt, always. Feel free to adopt anything that resonates with you, but always keep an eye on the mirror, both literally and metaphorically!

Silence and Solitude

If you've ever pictured the Buddha as the life of the party—you're in for a surprise. The EBTs paint him more as a hermit sage than a social butterfly. He often encouraged his followers to immerse themselves in the dharma and the serenity of silence rather than indulging in mundane rambling and unproductive discussions about topics like politics, material concerns, or the latest gossip.[1]

The Buddha compares the power of silence to a mighty stream, quietly weaving its way between rocks and crevices. This imagery stands in contrast to smaller creeks that thrash and splash about—a bit like the quiet confidence of a long-term investor versus the frenzied panic of a day trader. Those secured in themselves maintain their serenity, while others, like "half-empty pots," tend to make a lot of noise.[2]

Silence wasn't just a theoretical concept for the Buddha; it was his preferred method of communication. He often conveyed his thoughts and decisions through gestures and facial expressions. When he was asked to visit a severely ill monastic, he responded with a silent nod of agreement.[3] Invitations for meals from locals were met in the same manner.[4]

His quiet demeanor was so well known that when wanderers spotted him in the distance, they'd say, "Shh, quiet, don't make a sound. The Buddha likes quiet and praises it. Maybe he'll join us if we're also quiet."[5]

A king once visited a monastery where the Buddha stayed and marveled at the tranquil scene—a hall full of monastics deep in meditation. The sight left such an impression that he expressed a hope for his son to one day attain such inner peace.[6]

In some cultures, a woman's silence can be interpreted as a form of weakness or submissiveness. But understanding the

Buddha's practice of noble silence isn't just illuminating; it's empowering, especially for women who have been socially conditioned to believe otherwise. This isn't a silence born from oppression or inequality. Rather, it's mindful contemplation, a wellspring of strength and wisdom, not a sign of weakness or awkwardness.

This wisdom extends to knowing when to break that silence. The Buddha suggests that words, when spoken, should be like a soft, soothing melody—pleasing to the ear and warming to the heart.[7] But he recognizes that hard truths sometimes need airing. The key is waiting for the right moment to reveal them.[8] Speak the truth, but do so when it's constructive and beneficial, not just for the sake of being right.[9] Ultimately, when we choose to break the silence, our words should be truthful, timely, beneficial, concise, reasonable, and meaningful.[10]

This teaching resonates deeply with me, especially within the context of American culture, where speaking one's mind is often celebrated as a cornerstone of personal freedom and democracy. Learning to choose my words with care while also being outspoken in a constructive way has shaped me into someone who can stand firm in her convictions while fostering a harmonious environment. There are moments when I opt for silence, when it's not the right time to contribute. However, when my voice can serve as a bridge, enriching the conversation in a meaningful way, I don't hesitate to speak up.

It was one such moment that found me in a small, stuffy room at work, serving as a guest panelist for an advanced administrative support job interview. The atmosphere was a bit tense, laden with the seriousness of the task at hand: Two contenders. Identical interview scores. One, an out-of-state white candidate with specialized experience. The other, a local Black candidate with solid, transferable skills but no sector-specific experience.

After moments spent flipping through interview notes, the hiring manager, who was white, cautiously suggested, "The out-of-state candidate seems like a better fit."

I looked around. Heads were nodding from the other two white and Latine panel members. Yet an uneasy silence hung in the room, as if everyone was holding their breath. Time was ticking. I knew this was one of those moments when saying nothing would mean complicity in a decision that contradicted our organization's professed commitment to racial equity.

Summoning courage, I said, "If both candidates have identical scores and demonstrate the core skills to perform well in this role, shouldn't our organization's goal of advancing racial equity guide our decision toward the local candidate?"

Silence washed over the room again. But this silence was different—filled with contemplation and a reevaluation of assumptions. I went on to add that systemic factors often create uneven playing fields in areas such as education, employment, and housing. Therefore, the local candidate likely had more hurdles to clear.

The glances exchanged among the panel members were not just glances; they were affirmations, quiet nods to a truth they already knew. All of us had participated in the Seattle Race and Social Justice Initiative workshops, heeded the same calls from our leadership, and encountered these very principles in our organization's annual plans and reports. Yet, in that moment, I sensed a collective realization: the lofty ideals we'd often discussed were no longer abstract concepts; they were tangible actions unfolding right before us, ripe for application here and now.

In the end, we couldn't make a decision then and there. HR advised us to email our final choices separately for a more thorough review. Days passed. Then the word came: the local candidate was selected—unanimously.

This small victory didn't just put a smile on my face. I genuinely felt that it made a meaningful, if small, difference toward equalizing opportunities for underrepresented communities. It served as a reaffirmation of what can happen when we're guided by courage and clarity—when we choose to break our silence and advocate for what we believe in.

When Thích Nhất Hạnh formulated the term *engaged Buddhism*, he was addressing this duality: the balance between thoughtful silence and deliberate action. Between inner restraint and social advocacy. Between Eastern reflection and Western activism. Buddhism is not just a path for individual enlightenment but also a blueprint for societal well-being.

In this same thread, while the Buddha deeply valued moments of silence and solitude, his aim extended beyond personal growth; he envisioned a positive impact on society as a whole. Naturally, he found peace and contentment in the wilderness,[11] once musing, "In the still of high noon, when the birds have settled down, and the mighty jungle whispers to itself: that seems so delightful to me."[12] But these peaceful interludes were not idle; they were moments of deep meditation in which he both nurtured happiness in the present moment and planted seeds of compassion for future generations.[13] The Buddha hoped that if people saw how he and his disciples were able to find contentment and meaning living a simple life in harmony with nature, they might be inspired to tread a similar course.[14]

Reflecting on the ceaseless ebb and flow of time and existence, the Buddha painted a universe in constant flux, evolving through vast timescales, undergoing catastrophic ends and eventual regenerations.[15] He observed, "Who could ever imagine that the mountains will crumble, that the earth will transform, except for the one who has truly understood the nature of existence?"[16] With this expansive view of the universe, the Buddha endeavored to model a way of living that was in tune with the natural world—a minimalist, eco-conscious approach that prioritized balance over excess, wisdom over desire. He hoped that future generations would adopt this approach, viewing it not just as a spiritual ideal but as a viable route to a sustainable future, a path that honors the interdependence of all things.

There were times when the Buddha needed to "get away from it all," a bit like our cherished staycations today. He retreated into forests for weeks or months, interrupted only by those delivering his meals.[17] At other times, he'd set off on a solo trek, carrying nothing but his bowl and robe. His attendant Ānanda would remind everyone, "When the Buddha leaves like this, it means he wants to be alone."[18]

In today's COVID-19-impacted world, where the loss of Wi-Fi seems more catastrophic than the loss of solitude, the idea of extended alone time might seem a tad, well, lonesome. But for the Buddha, solitude is like a personal retreat, a haven for self-discovery and spiritual growth. He compares those who value solitude to a rhino's horn—solid, singular, and sturdy. He says if we find someone wise to accompany us, great! But if not, stride alone, courageous and free, like a lone elephant wandering in the wilderness.[19] Now, there's a certain American spirit to this, isn't there? Individualism, independence, and self-reliance—perhaps Buddhism isn't as foreign as it might initially appear!

The Buddha teaches that solitude empowers us to take an honest, hard look at ourselves, figure out what's holding us back, and set us on the path to progress.[20] He nudges us to try it out, even if the idea didn't immediately spark joy. For those who find the practice of solitude too daunting, he suggests a softer approach: practice with others but try to foster a sense of solitude within ourselves amid the company.[21]

He also distinguishes between those who crave social interaction and those who find happiness in solitude. He suggests that the latter group has an edge, more likely to find joy in letting go of worldly attachments, to find inner peace, and to achieve spiritual awakening without much difficulty.[22] These individuals are also more likely to reach significant spiritual milestones, like understanding their own minds and putting an end to suffering.[23]

Reflecting on my own experiences with the balance between social interaction and solitude, my mind returns to 2017. During my residential internship at a Zen monastery in El Paso, I found myself in a bustling microcosm: about forty monastics lived there, along with a constantly changing roster of lay residents and visitors. Additionally, the monastery's public mindfulness days attracted around two hundred people weekly. While the environment was undeniably enriching, it was also, paradoxically, draining. With kitchen duties, serving as staff at various retreats, teaching Vietnamese-English classes, and assisting with the composting, recycling, and garden watering of the nun's hamlet, my plate was more than full. Add to this a demanding daily practice regimen that began at the crack of dawn at five thirty and extended until the evening at seven, and the cumulative effect on my well-being became increasingly palpable. I felt an increasing need for a refuge of silence. So, by the second month, I requested to practice noble silence on Tuesdays to recharge my spiritual batteries.

The nuns approved my request at first, but they pulled a U-turn several weeks later. One of my mentors suggested my request was a little too "self-serving." Using hand gestures for communication had confused some nuns, and my silence disrupted the communal flow. "We want you to be one with the sangha. We want to be able to talk to you when we need to," she explained. She then proposed an alternative: if I felt the need to observe a full day of noble silence, then it would be more appropriate to do so on Mondays, which were already designated as "lazy days" at the monastery.

Mondays were free of structured activities, save for meals, and an evening hamlet "Happiness" meeting or a "Beginning Anew" meeting or ceremony. I often spent these mornings hiking with like-minded monastics, my fellow interns, and other lay practitioners, and then the afternoons composting and recycling alongside a nun. Agreeing to practice noble silence on such a day would restrict my engagement in these activities, thereby undermining my full participation in the community. It was a trade-off I found difficult to make, so with some reluctance, I chose to decline the offer.

The situation poses an intriguing paradox. Thích Nhất Hạnh, the Zen master who established the monastery, authored an entire book on the importance of silence, explaining how periods of silence are essential for both spiritual and mental well-being. He noted that many Plum Village practitioners embark on extended periods of noble silence, ranging from weeks to months. Furthermore, all his monasteries observe periods of noble silence from dusk till dawn. Yet, when I requested extending this practice to one full day a week for myself, it was seen by some of his disciples as incongruent with the community's ethos.

I share this experience to shine a light on a subtle observation: even in spiritual havens where wisdom flows freely, there can be a chasm between what's preached and what's practiced. This reflection is an invitation for open dialogue that fosters meaningful change. My earnest hope for spiritual leaders worldwide is that their actions be guided not by a focus on immediate concerns or communal conventions but by the timeless principles of compassion, understanding, and the profound teachings of the Buddha.

As for those navigating the hustle and bustle of everyday life, I pose this heart-to-self question: In the midst of our digitally saturated existence—where our attention is pulled by the unceasing dings of Zoom calls, emails, and social media alerts—what if we consciously set aside sanctuaries of silence in our busy schedule? What if we take some time to disconnect, dial down the noise of the world, and discover the wonders of solitude? Who knows what hidden treasures we might find in the quiet? We might stumble on a pleasant revelation—that life can be just as good, or even better, with the Wi-Fi switched off.

Nourishing Mind and Body

The Buddha may not be the first name that springs to mind when we think of wellness experts. But guess what? He had some advice on leading a healthy lifestyle—just ask King Pasenadi of Kosala, a royal foodie known for his love of rice and curries.

One day, the king waddled over to the Buddha, huffing and puffing, his belly still full from his latest feast. Observing the king's discomfort, the Buddha shared a nugget of wisdom: "Moderation and mindfulness in eating paves the way for a life of comfort and graceful aging."

This advice struck King Pasenadi like a ton of bricks. He was so moved that he instructed his attendant to recite this teaching before every meal. This daily reminder helped the king rethink his eating habits, regain control over his waistline, and discover the joy of savoring his food instead of gobbling it down. Grateful for the transformation, King Pasenadi became a vocal advocate of the Buddha's wisdom, crediting it for his newfound vitality and longevity.[24]

Fast-forward to today and modern dietitians echo the Buddha's enduring wisdom on mindful eating. They stress the importance of being aware of the taste, texture, and smell of our food, as well as acknowledging how we feel and think as we eat. By chewing slowly and recognizing when we're full, we can foster a healthier relationship with food. A 2020 article by Harvard Health Publishing supported the idea that mindful eating could contribute to weight reduction and overall health improvement.

One of my favorite mindful practices from the Plum Village Zen Tradition is the Five Contemplations before eating, which transform a simple meal into a profound spiritual experience:

1. This food is a gift of the earth, the sky, numerous living beings, and much hard and loving work.
2. May we eat with mindfulness and gratitude so as to be worthy to receive this food.
3. May we recognize and transform unwholesome mental formations, especially our greed, and learn to eat with moderation.
4. May we keep our compassion alive by eating in such a way that reduces the suffering of living beings, stops contributing to climate change, and heals and preserves our precious planet.
5. We accept this food so that we may nurture our brotherhood and sisterhood, build our Sangha, and nourish our ideal of serving all living beings.

In the EBTs, the Buddha demonstrated his mindful approach to food. He savored his food without experiencing greed for its taste. He ate simply to sustain his body, avoid harm, and support his spiritual practice, not for indulgence or physical appearance. Following each meal, he sat in quiet gratitude, neither criticizing the food nor expecting more.[25]

Moreover, he followed a unique eating schedule, partaking in just one meal per day—a practice he found beneficial for his well-being.[26] However, he offered flexibility to his followers. When a disciple, Bhaddāli, expressed concern, the Buddha suggested a compromise: eat part of the meal and save the leftovers for later.[27]

Beyond mere self-care, the Buddha's one-meal-a-day regimen also considered the well-being of the larger community. In those times, monastics depended on daily alms round for food. An influx of monastics could strain the local community. So by reducing the frequency of meals, the Buddha helped ensure that the monastic community did not overburden local generosity.

Fast-forward to 2023, in a vastly different setting—a pulsating Ed Sheeran concert in Seattle. Amid the crowd, I was struck by the visible prevalence of obesity, a complex health crisis that goes beyond mere numbers or statistics. It's a tangible, urgent issue with roots not only in diet and exercise but in overlooked elements like self-love and body positivity.

I've always held steadfast to the philosophy that loving oneself isn't merely about acceptance but active care. In fact, I view it as an act of empowerment, especially as a woman, challenging the societal narrative that often disguises dieting as body control rather than an exercise in self-care.

My commitment to self-care and conscious living has kept me at a consistent weight throughout my adult life, with a slight

105 pounds on a five-foot-three frame. During high school, my fondness for the daily cafeteria offerings of pizza, burgers, and fries nudged my weight to its peak of about 115 pounds. Yet when college began, and I took the helm in my kitchen, the anticipated "freshman 15" never materialized. Instead, I shed 10 pounds within months and have maintained that weight ever since.

I remember once, basking in the warm glow of a charming Italian bistro, a lighthearted comment from my date suggesting our lavish feast might pave the way to obesity. My reply was immediate, laced with unwavering certainty: "No, not me. I'm never going to be obese."

His eyebrows lifted. "You can't be sure of that."

I returned the gesture with an assured smile and said, "I am."

The conviction in my voice stems not from a place of arrogance but from an understanding of self-love rooted deeply in Buddhist teachings.

In a world that frequently confuses body positivity with unbridled indulgence, the Buddha's teachings offer a refreshing counterpoint. They don't just advocate for loving oneself but also for avoiding harm to oneself, whether through thought, word, or deed.[28]

Think about it like this: When we're in love, we don't intentionally hurt our partner, right? The same goes for the body we call home—our lifelong companion. So when I say, "I'm never going to be obese," it's not a shallow fixation on appearance. It's a vow of care and compassion toward my body, treating it with the gentle, loving consideration I would extend to someone I love.

Today's catchy slogans like "love yourself at any size" offer uplifting sentiments but often gloss over the complex conversation about what it means to truly care for oneself. While these messages encourage self-acceptance, they risk being misconstrued as justifications for neglecting our health under the guise of self-love. If we tell young people they can indulge without consequences, we might be ill-preparing them for future health implications. True self-love isn't an unconditional celebration of any state we find ourselves in but rather a balanced blend of embracing our present form and striving for optimal health. Our bodies aren't mere objects for display; they're living manifestations of our inner selves. Self-love, at its core, is an act of spiritual nurturing, setting the groundwork for the kindness we extend to ourselves and, by extension, to the world.

This emphasis on a mindful and balanced approach to self-care resonates with the principles found in the Buddha's teachings. Rather than indulging in sensory pleasures or self-neglect, the Buddha advocates for a middle path that nurtures both the body and spirit. He teaches that life's inherent suffering makes it even more imperative to strengthen our minds while we're physically healthy, essentially saying, "Make hay while the sun shines." By doing this, we don't just build physical resilience but cultivate a form of spiritual armor. This inner sanctuary allows us to weather life's inevitable storms with grace and equanimity.[29]

An extraordinary testament to the power of mind over physical suffering can be found in the story of the Venerable Thích Quảng Đức. It was 1963, a time marked by the South Vietnamese government's harsh treatment of Buddhists. To protest against this persecution, Thích Quảng Đức set himself on fire at a busy Sài Gòn intersection. As the flames danced around him, he sat calmly in the lotus position until his final breath. He showed us the tremendous potential of the human mind—strengthened through spiritual discipline—to transcend the most unimaginable physical pain.

you feel like causing harm. Remember, no matter where you go, the consequences of harmful actions will follow."[34] In this exchange, the Buddha's concern was twofold: caring for both the moral development of the boys and the well-being of the fish.

This universal compassion extended to his ethical stance on food and consumption. Contrary to some beliefs, although the Buddha allowed meat consumption, he by no means encouraged it, especially when an animal was killed solely for a monastic's meal. This reflects his foundational teaching that taking life—even for the sake of life—is ethically indefensible.[35]

The Buddha outlines five reasons why killing an animal for consumption inflicts harm: the initial order to capture the animal, the animal's distress when led by a leash, the act of execution itself, the animal's suffering during the ordeal, and the act of eating the meat that results from this sequence of pain.[36]

In the Buddha's time, due to harsh conditions and scarcity of food, he accepted any food offered during alms rounds. But it's reasonable to infer that, given the choice, he would likely have opted for a plant-based alternative, reflecting his profound compassion for all living beings.

This compassion is intricately linked to what the Buddha called the "four immeasurable minds." He advises, "Meditate on love. For when you meditate on love, any ill will be given up. Meditate on compassion. For when you meditate on compassion, any cruelty will be given up. Meditate on rejoicing. For when you meditate on rejoicing, any discontent will be given up. Meditate on equanimity. For when you meditate on equanimity, any repulsion will be given up."[37]

From a feminist and egalitarian viewpoint, these teachings possess transformative power. Love challenges patriarchal attitudes that have long belittled and disempowered women, opening the door to a more equitable space. Compassion is the antidote to discrimination, encouraging empathy toward marginalized communities. Rejoicing invites us to celebrate others' wins, a countermeasure to strategies that divide and disempower. Equanimity functions as a balancing force, useful for challenging biased norms and promoting equal opportunities for all.

If you're looking for a text that crystallizes these teachings, the *Metta Sutta* offers insights into the nature of love:

> Turn no one away, belittle no one,
> Let's not wish pain upon one another.
> Like a mother shielding her only child,
> Unfold a heart that's boundless for all beings.
> Radiate boundless love to the entire world—
> Unrestricted, without any hatred or enmity.[38]

To fully grasp the extent of the Buddha's compassion, consider the story of Aṅgulimāla. This notorious bandit, known for wearing his victims' fingers as necklaces, was feared by many. But he was the very person the Buddha chose to approach.

As Aṅgulimāla charged toward him, the Buddha maintained his composure, walking slowly and steadily. When Aṅgulimāla commanded him to halt, the Buddha calmly responded, "I have stopped, Aṅgulimāla. Now, it's your turn to do the same."

Puzzled, Aṅgulimāla frowned and asked, "What do you mean you've stopped?"

Looking into Aṅgulimāla's eyes, the Buddha said, "I have forever stopped—I've laid aside violence towards all creatures. But you, you continue to inflict harm. That's why I say: I have stopped, but you haven't."

Aṅgulimāla looked down at his weapons, his heart pounding as he considered the Buddha's words. For the first time, he saw his instruments of violence for what they truly were. With newfound clarity, he threw aside his weapons and sought refuge in the Buddha's teachings.

The Buddha extended a hand as he simply said, "Come, mendicant."

Thus began Aṅgulimāla's new life as a disciple, culminating in his eventual enlightenment. Reflecting on his transformative journey, he proclaimed:

> Someone whose bad deed
> is supplanted by the good,
> lights up the world,
> like the moon freed from a cloud.
>
> For irrigators guide the water,
> and fletchers straighten arrows;
> carpenters carve timber—
> but the astute tame themselves.
>
> Some tame by using the rod,
> some with goads, and some with whips.
> But the poised one tamed me
> without rod or sword.[39]

These tales shine a light on the empathetic essence of the Buddha's teachings and their profound potential for transformation. Through the story of Aṅgulimāla, we're reminded that the capacity for growth is within everyone, regardless of past deeds, gender, or societal roles. It's a poignant reminder that challenges the patriarchal notion that certain individuals—often women or stigmatized communities—are inherently limited by their circumstances. Aṅgulimāla's violent past had led his community to avoid him, much like how society shuns those it deems undesirable. But the Buddha, instead of reacting with fear or aversion, approached Aṅgulimāla with an open heart. He showed us that even those whom society condemns can change when met with understanding and compassion.

As we pivot to the last moments of the Buddha's life, this overarching theme of universal compassion finds vivid expression. Knowing that he had ingested a fatal meal from a blacksmith named Cunda, the Buddha turned his attention toward Cunda's potential suffering. He sought to comfort him, preemptively countering the blame and shame society might impose. He instructed Ānanda to assure Cunda that his offering held tremendous spiritual significance. Far from a tragic mistake, the meal marked the Buddha's transition from this transient world to the eternal peace of nirvāṇa.[40]

Even as he lay on his deathbed, the Buddha remained a dedicated teacher. He not only sought to comfort Cunda but also convened his disciples one last time to address any lingering doubts or uncertainties about his teachings. After triple-checking and finding no questions, he offered one final piece of advice: "All conditioned things are subject to decay. Persist with diligence."[41]

Reflecting on the Buddha's interactions with Aṅgulimāla and Cunda, we can also think about those often pushed to the margins of our society—individuals wrestling with mental health issues or substance abuse, carrying the weight of criminal records, or working in professions often stigmatized, like sex work. They are our modern-day Aṅgulimālas.

And then there are those who face societal biases—like immigrants and refugees, transgender individuals, or those experiencing homelessness; they are the Cundas of our time. In a society prone to bias and exclusion, the Buddha's teachings invite us to challenge our prejudices, to extend a hand of compassion to everyone, irrespective of gender, ethnicity, social standing, or even past misdeeds.

As we contemplate this inclusive approach, which urges us to overcome barriers and embrace forgiveness and understanding as cornerstones of community and personal growth, let's ask ourselves: Can we look beyond surface appearances and deeply ingrained stereotypes to see the unique human essence in everyone we meet? How often do we scrutinize our own actions, confronting the uncomfortable reality of any bias, prejudice, or indifference that may be lurking within us? What steps can we take to become more conscious and intentional in our interactions, creating spaces that not only allow but encourage transformation?

Whether you're nestled in the quiet suburbs or navigating the bustle of the city, the message remains the same: every meaningful journey starts with a single step—or, as in Aṅgulimāla's case, a single *stop*.

My earnest hope is that whenever life grants us the window of opportunity, each of us will seize that moment to take that step, make that stop, and weave compassion into every second of our lives to see the transformative power it holds—for ourselves, for others, and for our world we share.

ACKNOWLEDGMENTS

In the pages of this book, you have found not just my voice but also the echo of Adrienne Ingrum's belief in that voice. My deepest thanks to Adrienne for her unwavering support and insightful editorial guidance.

I am forever indebted to the rest of the Broadleaf Books team, whose dedication and creative passion have turned my manuscript into the realized dream that now accompanies you.

To my literary agent, Leticia Gomez, whose leap of faith illuminated my path when the way forward was but a haze. Her tenacious spirit and nurturing mentorship have been invaluable.

To my parents, my inspiration—Trần Đại Trình and Đỗ Thị Sương—whose selfless and unconditional love knows no bounds. I carry the pride of being your daughter like a crown.

To my siblings: Chân Như and anh Tuân, Ý Thanh and anh Tuấn, Khánh Linh and anh Sơn, Bích Thu, Nhật Quang, and Bảo Trân—I adore you all so much. Long live the Trần dynasty!

To my nieces and nephews: Thảo and Tân, Anh, Duy, Tú, Thi, Thư, Acelyn, Aurora, Aria, and Keanu—your laughter and dreams inspire my every sentence.

Profound thanks to my earliest readers, remarkable individuals who, amid their full and vibrant lives, have generously given their precious time to my pages: Eileen Keira, Erin Okuno, Holly J. Hughes, Inger Brinck, Jeremy Sherman, Julie Phạm,

Lisa Manterfield, Melissa Muir, Nathan Bombardier, Norea Hoeft, Susan Liễu, and Vủ Lê.

To the quiet cheerleaders in my life: Andrew Scoggin, Anh Cường, Brother Birkenstock, Brother Blissley, Brother Coconut, Brother Flowsensei, Brother Noodley, Brother Quillar, Brother Sandcastle, Brother Snowcast, Brother Solespirit, Brother Strummer, Brother Sunstone, Brother Tamales, Claudia Gross-Shader, Cora Stoltenberg, Cúc Vũ, David Jones, Gary Ireland, Gary Lý, Hany Amy, Hinh Trần, Hùng Trần, IB Osuntoki, Jessica Hong, Jerphy Lee, Katie Truelove, Khiêm Nhường Nguyễn, Khôi Nguyễn, Khuê Nguyễn, Laura Bet, Luna Verrine, Marc Stepper, Melissa Alderson, Nhật Trần, Paul Tamura, Phil Chang, Phương Đỗ, Ramu Ponneganti, Rich Cook, Rodney Outlaw, Sarah Bland, Sarah Valenta, Shirin Yim Leos, Sister Gemstone, Sister Inkwise, Sister Lenslively, Sister Lunarfae, Sister Melodist, Sister Mononoke, Sister Oasis, Sister Scriptguard, Sister Glaze, Sister Sprout, Susan Davis, Tâm Định, Tejas Bhosale, Thái Hòa Nguyễn, Thanh Tân, Thầy Thích Quảng Thuyết, Thiện Tín Trường, Trí Khúc, Trí Nguyễn, Vinícius Jarina, Yogesh Sharma, Yuvanesh Murugesan, and the members of Thảnh Thơi Sangha, Cherry Blossom Sangha, and my launch team—each of you holds a special place in my heart.

And to you, readers, thank you for turning these pages and coming this far. Though I've aimed for accuracy, I take ownership of any missteps and see them as opportunities for growth. Some details have been modified for privacy, but the essence of this book is my lived truth. May it spark a light within you to share your own story as we strive to transform the walls of the past into the bridges of the future.

NOTES

Chapter 1

1 MN 115 (Bahudhātuka Sutta), AN 1.279 (Dutiya Vagga).
2 AN 5.229 (Paṭhamakaṇhasappa Sutta).
3 AN 3.131 (Paṭicchanna Sutta).

Chapter 2

1 SN 1.46 (Accharā Sutta).
2 AN 5.122 (Satisūpaṭṭhita Sutta).
3 MN 73 (Mahāvaccha Sutta).
4 AN 8.49 (Paṭhamaidhalokika Sutta).
5 MN 68 (Naḷakapāna Sutta).
6 AN 6.16 (Nakulapitu Sutta).
7 DN 33 (Saṅgīti Sutta).
8 MN 27 (Cūḷahatthipadopama Sutta), MN 51 (Kandaraka Sutta).
9 Thig 6.3 Khematherigatha, Thig 1.17 (Dhammā Therīgāthā), Thig 2.3 (Sumaṅgalamātā Therīgāthā), Thig 5.6 (Mittākāḷī Therīgāthā), Thig 5.10 (Paṭācārā Therīgāthā), Thig 13.4 (Sundarī Therīgāthā).
10 SN 10.11 (Cīrā Sutta), SN 10.10 (Dutiyasukkā Sutta), Thig 5.9 (Bhaddākuṇḍalakesā Therīgāthā).
11 Thig 16.1 (Sumedhā Therīgāthā), Thig 12.1 (Puṇṇā Therīgāthā), Thig 13.2 (Rohinī Therīgāthā), Thig 2.4 (Aḍḍhakāsi Therīgāthā), Thig 6.4 (Sujātā Therīgāthā).
12 Thig 13.5 (Subhākammāradhītu Therīgāthā), Thig 6.2 (Vāseṭṭhī Therīgāthā), Thig 5.5 (Nanduttarā Therīgāthā), Thig 7.2 (Cālā Therīgāthā), Thig 5.8 (Soṇā Therīgāthā), Thig 2.9 (Abhayā Therīgāthā),

Thig 2.10 (Sāmā Therīgāthā), Thig 3.1 (Aparāsāmā Therīgāthā), Thig 6.5 (Anopamā Therīgāthā), Thig 6.6 (Mahāpajāpatigotamī Therīgāthā).

13 Thig 3.5 (Ubbiri Therīgāthā), Thig 3.3 (Aparāuttamā Therīgāthā), Thig 2.2 (Jentā Therīgāthā), Thig 1.15 (Uttarā Therīgāthā), Thig 1.16 (Vuḍḍhapabbajitasumanā Therīgāthā), Thig 2.8 (Abhayamātu Therīgāthā), Thig 5.4 (Sundarīnandā Therīgāthā), Thig 10.1 (Kisāgotamī Therīgāthā), Thig 4.1 (Bhaddākāpilānī Therīgāthā).

14 Thig 3.2 (Uttamā Therīgāthā), Thig 2.5 (Cittā Therīgāthā), Thig 3.7 (Selā Therīgāthā), Thig 6.8 (Vijayā Therīgāthā), Thig 7.3 (Upacālā Therīgāthā), Thig 8.1 (Sīsūpacālā Therīgāthā), Thig 5.2 (Vimalā Therīgāthā), Thig 5.7 (Sakulā Therīgāthā), Thig 5.12 (Candā Therīgāthā), Thig 7.1 (Uttarā Therīgāthā), Thig 9.1 (Vaḍḍhamātu Therīgāthā), Thig 2.6 (Mettikā Therīgāthā), Thig 11.1 (Uppalavaṇṇā Therīgāthā).

15 Thig 6.1 (Pañcasatamattā Therīgāthā).

16 MN 44 (Cūḷavedalla Sutta).

17 MN 115 (Bahudhātukasutta).

18 AN 8.85 (Samaṇa Sutta).

19 AN 7.56 (Tissabrahmā Sutta).

20 MN 98 (Vāseṭṭha Sutta).

21 SN 18.22 (Apagata Sutta).

22 SN 5.2 (Somā Sutta).

23 SN 22.64 (Maññamāna Sutta).

Chapter 3

1 Thig 14.1 (Subhā Jīvakambavanikā Therīgāthā).

2 SN 35.127 (The Bhāradvāja Sutta).

3 SN 1.34 (Nasanti Sutta).

4 AN 2.21–31 (Bāla Vagga).

5 Ud 4.1 (Meghiya Sutta).

6 AN 7.36 (Paṭhamamitta Sutta).

7 AN 7.37 (Dutiyamitta Sutta).

8 Ud 6.2 (Sattajaṭila Sutta).

9 AN 4.55 (Paṭhamasamajīvī Sutta).

10 DN 31 (Siṅgāla Sutta).

Chapter 4

1 MN 93 (Assalāyana Sutta).
2 MN 38 (Mahā Taṇhāsaṅkhaya Sutta).
3 SN 23.2 (Satta Sutta).
4 SN 5.10 (Vajirā Sutta).
5 SN 12.12 (Moḷiyaphagguna Sutta).
6 SN 22.3 (Hāliddikāni Sutta).
7 SN 12.64 (Atthirāga Sutta).
8 DN 15 (Mahānidāna Sutta).
9 SN 56.48 (Dutiyachiggaḷayuga Sutta).
10 DN 16 (Mahāparinibbāna Sutta).
11 Ud 2.9 (Visākhā Sutta).
12 SN 1.19 (Kuṭikā Sutta).

Chapter 5

1 Bu Pj 1 (Methuna Dhamma).
2 Mil 3.6.2 (Sabbaññūbhāvapañha).
3 Thag 17.3 (Ānanda Theragāthā).
4 SN 47.9 (Gilāna Sutta).
5 Kd 21 Pañcasatikakkhandhaka.
6 Kp 5 (Maṅgala Sutta), Snp 2.4 (Maṅgala Sutta).
7 AN 2.33 (Samacitta Vagga).
8 AN 5.58 (Licchavikumāraka Sutta).
9 Snp 2.14 (Dhammika Sutta).
10 Dhp 332.
11 AN 3.45 (Paṇḍita Sutta).
12 MN 81 (Ghaṭikāra Sutta).
13 Kp 5 (Maṅgala Sutta).
14 AN 3.31 (Sabrahmaka Sutta).
15 SN 12.37 (Natumha Sutta), SN 12.41 (Pañcaverabhaya Sutta).
16 SN 1.17 (Dukkara Sutta).
17 Dhp 50.
18 MN 12 (Mahāsīhanāda Sutta).
19 Iti 47 (Jāgariya Sutta).

20 AN 8.58 (Dutiyaāhuneyya Sutta).
21 Dhp 215.
22 AN 2.20 (Adhikaraṇa Vagga), AN 5.155 (Dutiyasaddhammasammosa Sutta), AN 5.156 (Tatiyasaddhammasammosa Sutta), SN 47.25 (Aññatarabrāhmaṇa Sutta), SN 47.22 (Ciraṭṭhiti Sutta), SN 47.23 (Parihāna Sutta), Dhp 364, Dhp 367, AN 6.84 (Rattidivasa Sutta), AN 10.86 (Adhimāna Sutta), Iti 45 (Paṭisallāna Sutta), Iti 86 (Dhammānudhammapaṭipanna Sutta), SN 35.96 (Parihānadhamma Sutta), SN 46.25 (Aparihāniya Sutta), Iti 79 (Parihāna Sutta), AN 7.24 (Dutiyasattaka Sutta), AN 7.25 (Tatiyasattaka Sutta), SN 16.7 (Dutiyaovāda Sutta), AN 7.26 (Bojjhaṅga Sutta), AN 7.27 (Saññā Sutta), AN 10.14 (Cetokhila Sutta), AN 10.67 (Paṭhamanaḷakapāna Sutta), AN 7.28 (Paṭhamaparihāni Sutta), AN 8.79 (Parihāna Sutta), AN 7.32 (Appamādagārava Sutta), AN 7.33 (Hirigārava Sutta), AN 7.34 (Paṭhamasovacassatā Sutta), AN 7.29 (Dutiyaparihāni Sutta), AN 6.21 (Sāmaka Sutta), AN 6.22 (Aparihāniya Sutta), AN 6.31 (Sekha Sutta), AN 6.32 (Paṭhamaaparihāna Sutta), AN 6.33 (Dutiyaaparihāna Sutta), AN 6.69 (Devatā Sutta).
23 AN 5.154 (Paṭhamasaddhammasammosa Sutta).
24 SN 16.13 (Saddhammappatirūpaka Sutta), AN 7.59 (Kimila Sutta), AN 6.40 (Kimila Sutta), AN 5.201 (Kimila Sutta), DN 34 (Dasuttara Sutta).
25 AN 1.114–131 (Dutiyapamādādi Vagga).
26 DN 34 (Dasuttara Sutta).
27 AN 7.23 (Paṭhamasattaka Sutta).
28 AN 10.84 (Byākaraṇa Sutta).
29 SN 20.7 (Āṇi Sutta).

Chapter 6

1 MN 26 (Pāsarās Sutta).
2 DN 29 (Pāsādika Sutta).
3 AN 5.230 (Dutiyakaṇhasappa Sutta).

Chapter 7

1 DN 28 (Sampasādanīya Sutta).
2 MN 149 (Mahāsaḷāyatanika Sutta).

3 Ud 3.10 (Loka Sutta), Iti 77 (Bhidura Sutta), SN 22.94 (Puppha Sutta).
4 SN 55.5 (Dutiyasāriputta Sutta).
5 MN 22 (Alagaddūpama Sutta), MN 68 (Naḷakapāna Sutta).
6 SN 55.4 (Paṭhamasāriputta Sutta), AN 9.27 (Paṭhamavera Sutta), DN 33 (Saṅgīti Sutta).
7 DN 16 (Mahāparinibbāna Sutta).
8 MN 75 (Māgaṇḍiya Sutta).
9 MN 106 (Āneñjasappāya Sutta).
10 Iti 45 (Paṭisallāna Sutta).
11 Dhp 372.
12 MN 122 (Mahāsuññata Sutta).
13 AN 4.41 (Samādhibhāvanā Sutta).
14 DN 33 (Saṅgīti Sutta).
15 MN 122 (Mahāsuññata Sutta).
16 MN 7 (Vattha Sutta), SN 46.54 (Mettā Sahagata Sutta).
17 AN 6.10 (Mahānāma Sutta).
18 MN 10 (Mahāsatipaṭṭhāna Sutta).
19 SN 1.18 (Hirī Sutta), SN 35.247 (Chappāṇakopama Sutta), Ud 3.5 (Mahāmoggallāna Sutta).
20 SN 54.8 (Padīpopama Sutta).
21 Ud 1.10 (Bāhiya Sutta).
22 SN 35.95 (Mālukyaputta Sutta).
23 AN 4.61 (Pattakamma Sutta).
24 AN 7.52 (Dānamahapphala Sutta), AN 8.33 (Dānavatthu Sutta).
25 AN 11.11 (Paṭhamamahānāma Sutta).
26 AN 6.37 (Chaḷaṅgadāna Sutta).
27 MN 103 (Kinti Sutta), AN 8.19 (Pahārāda Sutta), AN 7.71 (Bhāvanā Sutta), SN 45.155 (Ākāsa Sutta), SN 22.101 (Vāsijaṭa Sutta), SN 22.81 (Pālileyya Sutta).
28 AN 6.30 (Anuttariya Sutta).
29 AN 7.45 (Samādhiparikkhāra Sutta), SN 45.28 (Samādhi Sutta).
30 MN 112 (Chabbisodhana Sutta), MN 125 (Dantabhūmi Sutta).
31 AN 3.87 (Dutiyasikkhā Sutta).
32 Snp 1.12 (Muni Sutta).
33 Ud 2.1 (Mucalinda Sutta), Dhp 354.
34 DN 16 (Mahāparinibbāna Sutta).

35 MN 139 (Araṇavibhaṅga Sutta), Cullavaga, Vin. II, 139.
36 DN 16 (Mahāparinibbāna Sutta).
37 SN 4.5 (Dutiyamārapāsa Sutta).

Chapter 8

1 Snp 2.14 (Dhammika Sutta).
2 AN 8.41 (Saṁkhittūposatha Sutta).
3 AN 5.177 (Vaṇijjā Sutta).
4 MN 51 (Kandaraka Sutta).
5 SN 55.7 (Veḷudvāreyya Sutta).
6 Dhp 129 and 130.
7 Ud 5.1 (Piyatara Sutta).
8 SN 3.4 (Piya Sutta), AN 8.29 (Akkhaṇa Sutta).
9 MN 13 (Mahādukkhakkhandha Sutta), DN 15 (Mahānidāna Sutta).
10 Snp 4.15 (Attadaṇḍa Sutta).
11 MN 21 (Kakacūpama Sutta).
12 SN 42.3 (Yodhājīva Sutta).
13 SN 11.10 (Samuddaka Sutta), Dhp 1 and 2.
14 SN 36.21 (Sīvaka Sutta).
15 DN 5 (Kūṭadanta Sutta).
16 AN 3.14 (Cakkavatti Sutta).
17 AN 10.92 (Bhaya Sutta).
18 SN 45.7 (Dutiyaaññatarabhikkhu Sutta).
19 MN 128 (Upakkilesa Sutta).

Chapter 9

1 AN 4.61 (Pattakamma Sutta), AN 5.174 (Vera Sutta).
2 MN 114 (Sevitabbasevitabba Sutta), MN 41 (Saleyyaka Sutta), AN 10.176 (Cunda Sutta).
3 MN 73 (Mahāvaccha Sutta).
4 Snp 4.14 (Tuvaṭaka Sutta).
5 MN 18 (Madhupiṇḍika Sutta).
6 MN 64 (Mahāmālukya Sutta).
7 AN 6.104 (Atammaya Sutta).

8 MN 69 (Goliyāni Sutta).
9 DN 27 (Aggañña Sutta).
10 AN 7.51 (Saṁyoga Sutta).
11 AN 3.57 (Vacchagotta Sutta).
12 AN 8.19 (Pahārāda Sutta).

Chapter 10

1 SN 10.12 (Āḷavaka Sutta).
2 AN 7.52 (Dānamahapphala Sutta), AN 8.33 (Dānavatthu Sutta).
3 Iti 26 (Dāna Sutta).
4 Iti 75 (Avuṭṭhika Sutta).
5 SN 20.4 (Okkhā Sutta), AN 8.1 (Mettā Sutta), AN 9.18 (Navaṅguposatha Sutta).
6 SN 20.3 (Kula Sutta), AN 11.15 (Mettā Sutta).
7 SN 36.31 (Nirāmisa Sutta), SN 42.13 (Pāṭaliya Sutta), SN 46.26 (Taṇhakkhaya Sutta).
8 Snp 3.6 (Sabhiya Sutta).
9 MN 54 (Potaliya Sutta).
10 DN 29 (Pāsādika Sutta), AN 9.7 (Sutavā Sutta), Snp 1.11 (Vijaya Sutta), Snp 4.14 (Tuvaṭaka Sutta).
11 AN 7.49 (Dutiyasaññā Sutta), Snp 1.9 (Hemavata Sutta), SN 1.20 (Samiddhi Sutta).
12 AN 4.153 (Paññābala Sutta).
13 AN 4.256 (Saṅgahavatthu Sutta).
14 AN 6.44 (Migasālā Sutta).
15 AN 4.20 (Bhattuddesaka Sutta).
16 AN 6.76 (Arahatta Sutta).
17 Snp 4.9 (Māgaṇḍiya Sutta).
18 Snp 4.5 (Paramaṭṭhaka Sutta).
19 DN 25 (Udumbarika Sutta), DN 33 (Saṅgīti Sutta), MN 4 (Bhayabherava Sutta), MN 15 (Anumāna Sutta).
20 DN 2 (Sāmaññaphala Sutta).
21 Thag 14.2 (Godatta Tthera Gāthā).
22 Snp 1.12 (Muni Sutta).
23 SN 17.5 (Mīḷhaka Sutta).

Chapter 11

1 AN 5.202 (Dhammassavana Sutta).
2 Ja 63 (Takka Jātaka).
3 SN 11.10 (Samuddaka Sutta).
4 Dhp 165.
5 SN 3.20 (Dutiyaaputtaka Sutta).
6 SN 55.43 (Tatiyaabhisanda Sutta).
7 AN 8.39 (Abhisanda Sutta).
8 Iti 27 (Mettābhāvanā Sutta).
9 Dhp 50.
10 DN 21 (Sakkapañha Sutta).
11 DN 16 (Mahāparinibbāna Sutta).
12 AN 8.26 (Jīvaka Sutta).
13 SN 41.1 (Saṁyojana Sutta).
14 MN 40 (Cūḷaassapura Sutta).
15 Ud 4.2 (Uddhata Sutta).
16 AN 8.9 (Nanda Sutta).
17 DN 29 (Pāsādika Sutta).
18 Dhp 187.
19 MN 143 (Anāthapiṇḍikovāda Sutta).
20 SN 7.7 (Suddhika Sutta), SN 1.81 (Araṇa Sutta).
21 MN 90 (Kaṇṇakatthala Sutta), SN 7.9 (Sundarika Sutta).
22 SN 47.9 (Gilāna Sutta).
23 Dhp 72–74.
24 AN 10.45 (Rājantepurappavesana Sutta).
25 Ud 2.2 (Rāja Sutta).
26 MN 86 (Aṅgulimāla Sutta), Thag 12.2 (Sunītat Theragāthā), SN 12.70 (Susimaparibbājaka Sutta), DN 16 (Mahāparinibbāna Sutta), Thig 5.12 (Candā Therīgāthā).
27 Thig 5.9 (Bhaddā Kuṇḍalakesā Therīgāthā).
28 MN 95 (Caṅkī Sutta).
29 AN 3.65 (Kesamutti Sutta).
30 Thig 5.8 (Soṇā Therīgāthā).
31 Thig 3.2 (Uttamā Therīgāthā).
32 Thig 6.8 (Vijayā Therīgāthā).

33 Thig 7.1 (Uttarā Therīgāthā).
34 Thi Ap 35 (Sukkātherīa Padāna).
35 Thig 5.11 (Tiṁsamattā Therīgāthā).
36 SN 18.22 (Apagata Sutta).
37 SN 1.34 (Nasanti Sutta).
38 SN 1.25 (Arahanta Sutta).
39 AN 9.5 (Bala Sutta).
40 AN 4.7 (Sobhana Sutta).
41 AN 5.30 (Nāgita Sutta), SN 17.10 (Sagāthaka Sutta), Ud 1.4 (Huṁhuṅka Sutta).
42 MN 47 (Vīmaṁsaka Sutta), MN 56 (Upāli Sutta), DN 24 (Pāthika Sutta), MN 7 (Vattha Sutta).
43 MN 122 (Mahāsuññata Sutta), AN 7.83 (Satthusāsana Sutta), SN 56.8 (Cintasutta), MN 72 (Aggivaccha Sutta), DN 29 (Pāsādika Sutta), DN 9 (Poṭṭhapāda Sutta).
44 AN 6.10 (Mahānāma Sutta), MN 7 (Vattha Sutta), DN 24 (Pāthika Sutta), DN 19 (Mahāgovinda Sutta).
45 MN 7 (Vattha Sutta).
46 Dhp 354, AN 9.5 (Bala Sutta), Iti 98 (Dāna Sutta).
47 AN 9.5 (Bala Su tta).
48 AN 2.41 (Samacitta Vagga).
49 MN 139 (Araṇavibhaṅga Sutta).
50 SN 1.38 (Sakalika Sutta).
51 MN 45 (Cūḷadhammasamādāna Sutta).
52 Snp 2.11 (Rāhula Sutta).
53 SN 18.21 (Anusaya Sutta).
54 Kp 6 (Ratana Sutta).
55 AN 7.49 (Dutiyasaññā Sutta).
56 DN 31 (Siṅgāla Sutta).
57 AN 10.13 (Saṁyojana Sutta).
58 SN 12.22 (Dutiyadasabala Sutta), MN 39 (Mahāassapura Sutta).
59 Snp 4.10 (Purābheda Sutta).
60 MN 74 (Dīghanakha Sutta), Ud 5.3 (Suppabuddhakuṭṭhi Sutta).
61 SN 47.9 (Gilāna Sutta).
62 MN 70 (Kīṭāgiri Sutta).
63 Dhp 239.

64 AN 8.20 (Uposatha Sutta).
65 AN 2.5 (Kammakaraṇa Vagga).
66 AN 3.74 (Nigaṇṭha Sutta).
67 Snp 4.9 (Māgaṇḍiya Sutta).
68 SN 8.2 (Aratī Sutta).
69 Ud 4.4 (Yakkhapahāra Sutta).
70 MN 47 (Vīmaṁsaka Sutta).
71 AN 8.71 (Paṭhamasaddhā Sutta), AN 8.72 (Dutiyasaddhā Sutta), SN 35.155 (Dhammakathikapuccha Sutta).
72 AN 10.18 (Dutiyanātha Sutta).
73 AN 5.194 (Kāraṇapālī Sutta).
74 SN 47.9 (Gilāna Sutta).
75 SN 1.81 (Araṇa Sutta).

Chapter 12

1 MN 90 (Kaṇṇakatthala Sutta).
2 SN 12.61 (Assutavā Sutta), SN 12.20 (Paccaya Sutta), SN 55.28 (Paṭhamabhayaverūpasanta Sutta), Ud 1.1 (Paṭhamabodhi Sutta).
3 SN 47.9 (Gilāna Sutta).
4 DN 16 (Mahāparinibbāna Sutta).
5 Ud 8.5 (Cunda Sutta).
6 MN 36 (Mahāsaccaka Sutta).
7 MN 31 (Cūḷagosiṅga Sutta).
8 SN 35.243 (Avassutapariyāya Sutta).
9 AN 6.42 (Nāgita Sutta).
10 SN 7.13 (Devahita Sutta).
11 SN 48.41 (Jarādhamma Sutta).
12 DN 28 (Sampasādanīya Sutta).
13 DN 11 (Kevaṭṭa Sutta).
14 DN 24 (Pāthika Sutta).
15 SN 12.70 (Susimaparibbājaka Sutta).
16 SN 22.4 (Dutiyahāliddikāni Sutta).
17 MN 112 (Chabbisodhana Sutta).
18 AN 6.29 (Udāyī Sutta).
19 AN 6.30 (Anuttariya Sutta).

20 SN 35.81 (Sambahulabhikkhu Sutta), SN 45.5 (Kimatthiya Sutta), SN 12.43 (Dukkha Sutta).
21 SN 51.15 (Uṇṇābhabrāhmaṇa Sutta), Iti 15 (Taṇhāsaṁyojana Sutta), MN 74 (Dīghanakha Sutta).
22 SN 54.11 (Icchānaṅgala Sutta), SN 1.28 (Mahaddhana Sutta), AN 5.170 (Bhaddaji Sutta), MN 73 (Mahāvaccha Sutta), MN 107 (Gaṇakamoggallāna Sutta).
23 SN 38.1 (Nibbānapañhā Sutta), SN 45.36 (Dutiyasāmañña Sutta), SN 45.6 (Paṭhamaaññatarabhikkhu Sutta), SN 45.7 (Dutiyaaññatarabhikkhu Sutta).
24 AN 7.83 (Satthusāsana Sutta), MN 83 (Maghadeva Sutta), DN 25 (Udumbarika Sutta).
25 MN 131 (Bhaddekaratta Sutta).
26 DN 30 (Lakkhaṇa Sutta), MN 91 (Brahmāyu Sutta), MN 92 (Sela Sutta).
27 MN 91 (Brahmāyu Sutta).
28 MN 140 (Dhātuvibhaṅga Sutta).
29 DN 2 (Sāmaññaphala Sutta).
30 MN 96 (Esukārī Sutta).
31 SN 47.11 (Mahāpurisa Sutta).
32 Snp 5.3 (Tissa Metteyya Māṇavapucchā).
33 DN 1 (Brahmajāla Sutta).
34 Snp 2.13 (Sammāparibbājanīya Sutta).
35 SN 22.43 (Attadīpa Sutta).
36 Dhp 276.
37 DN 25 (Udumbarika Sutta).
38 MN 82 (Raṭṭhapāla Sutta).
39 AN 3.61 (Titthāyatana Sutta).
40 SN 7.18 (Kaṭṭhahāra Sutta).
41 AN 4.45 (Rohitassa Sutta), SN 45.163 (Āsava Sutta).
42 AN 10.13 (Saṁyojana Sutta), SN 45.180 (Uddhambhāgiya Sutta), SN 50.99–108 (Punaogha Vagga).
43 Snp 4.9 (Māgaṇḍiya Sutta), Snp 4.13 (Mahābyūha Sutta).
44 Snp 4.5 (Paramaṭṭhaka Sutta).
45 SN 6.6 (Brahmaloka Sutta).
46 Snp 5.4 (Puṇṇaka Maṇava Puccha).

47 SN 42.6 (Asibandhakaputta Sutta).
48 Snp 2.9 (Kiṁsīla Sutta).
49 Dhp 19.
50 SN 7.7 (Suddhika Sutta).

Chapter 13

1 DN 14 (Mahāpadāna Sutta).

Chapter 14

1 DN 21 (Sakkapañha Sutta).
2 SN 56.104 (Manussacutipettivisaya Sutta), AN 8.29 (Akkhaṇa Sutta).
3 Dhp 182.
4 AN 8.29 (Akkhaṇa Sutta).
5 SN 12.37 (Natumha Sutta).
6 Iti 40 (Vijjā Sutta).
7 AN 3.65 (Kesamutti Sutta).
8 MN 41 (Sāleyyaka Sutta).
9 Dhp 115 and 103.

Chapter 15

1 MN 122 (Mahāsuññata Sutta).
2 Snp 3.11 (Nālaka Sutta).
3 AN 6.56 (Phagguna Sutta).
4 AN 5.143 (Sārandada Sutta), MN 53 (Sekha Sutta).
5 DN 25 (Udumbarika Sutta).
6 DN 2 (Sāmaññaphala Sutta).
7 AN 10.99 (Upāli Sutta), MN 114 (Sevitabbāsevitabba Sutta).
8 MN 139 (Araṇavibhaṅga Sutta).
9 MN 58 (Abhayarājakumāra Sutta).
10 AN 5.198 (Vācā Sutta), AN 10.99 (Upāli Sutta).
11 Dhp 305.
12 SN 1.15 (Saṇamāna Sutta).
13 MN 4 (Bhayabherava Sutta).

14 SN 16.5 (Jiṇṇa Sutta).
15 DN 27 (Aggañña Sutta).
16 AN 7.66 (Sattasūriya Sutta).
17 SN 45.11 (Paṭhamavihāra Sutta), SN 54.9 (Vesālī Sutta), SN 45.12 (Dutiyavihāra Sutta).
18 SN 22.81 (Pālileyya Sutta), Ud 4.5 (Nāga Sutta).
19 Snp 1.3 (Khaggavisāṇa Sutta), condensed.
20 Iti 38 (Vitakka Sutta).
21 SN 6.13 (Andhakavinda Sutta).
22 MN 122 (Mahāsuññata Sutta).
23 AN 6.68 (Saṅgaṇikārāma Sutta).
24 SN 3.13 (Donapaka Sutta).
25 MN 91 (Brahmāyu Sutta).
26 MN 70 (Kīṭāgiri Sutta), AN 10.99 (Upāli Sutta), AN 5.228 (Ussūrabhatta Sutta), MN 112 (Chabbisodhana Sutta).
27 MN 65 (Bhaddāli Sutta).
28 SN 3.4 (Piya Sutta), AN 8.29 (Akkhaṇa Sutta).
29 AN 5.78 (Dutiyaanāgatabhaya Sutta).
30 AN 9.4 (Nandaka Sutta).
31 AN 4.111 (Kesi Sutta).
32 SN 22.87 (Vakkali Sutta).
33 SN 22.84 (Tissa Sutta).
34 Ud 5.4 (Kumāraka Sutta).
35 AN 8.12 (Sīha Sutta).
36 MN 55 (Jīvaka Sutta).
37 MN 62 (Mahārāhulovāda Sutta).
38 Kp 9 (Mettā Sutta), condensed.
39 MN 86 (Aṅgulimāla Sutta).
40 Ud 8.5 (Cunda Sutta), DN 16 (Mahāparinibbāna Sutta).
41 DN 16 (Mahāparinibbāna Sutta).

FURTHER READING

Adichie, Chimamanda Ngozi. *We Should All Be Feminists*. Paperback. Knopf Doubleday Publishing Group, 2015. ISBN: 9781101911761, 110191176X.

Finnigan, Mary, and Rob Hogendoorn. *Sex and Violence in Tibetan Buddhism: The Rise and Fall of Sogyal Rinpoche*. Jorvik Press, 2019.

Harvey, Brian Peter, ed. *Common Buddhist Text: Guidance and Insight from the Buddha*. Mahachulalongkornrajavidyalaya University Press, 2017. ISBN: 9786163003201, 6163003209.

Khema, Ayya. *Be an Island: The Buddhist Practice of Inner Peace*. Paperback. Wisdom Publications, 1999. ISBN: 9780861711475, 0861711475.

Không, Sister Chân. *Learning True Love: Practicing Buddhism in a Time of War*. E-book. ReadHowYouWant, 2008. ISBN: 9781458711335, 1458711331.

Nhật Từ, Thích. *423 Lời Vàng Của Phật (Kinh Pháp Cú)*. E-book. Tủ sách Đạo Phật Ngày Nay, 2016. ISBN: 9786048688110, 6048688113. Language: Vietnamese.

Nhất Hạnh, Thích. *Fragrant Palm Leaves: Journals, 1962–1966*. Paperback. Penguin Publishing Group, 1999. ISBN: 9781573227964, 157322796X.

Nhất Hạnh, Thích. *Old Path White Clouds*. Paperback. ReadHowYouWant, 2010. ISBN: 9781458768254, 1458768252.

Rahula, Walpola. *What the Buddha Taught: Revised and Expanded Edition with Texts from Suttas and Dhammapada*. e-book. Grove Atlantic, 2007. ISBN: 9780802198105, 0802198104.

Salzberg, Sharon. *Lovingkindness: The Revolutionary Art of Happiness*. e-book. Shambhala, 2020. ISBN: 9780834842731, 0834842734.

SuttaCentral Editions. Translated by Bhikkhu Sujato. Includes ten books such as *The Long Discourses (Dīgha Nikāya)* and *The Middle Discourses (Majjhima Nikāya)*. Available in multiple formats. Lulu, accessed September 17, 2023. https://suttacentral.net/editions?lang=en.

Wright, Robert. *Why Buddhism Is True: The Science and Philosophy of Meditation and Enlightenment*. Simon and Schuster, 2017.

INDEX

ABOUT THE AUTHOR

Nhi Yến Đỗ Trần immigrated with her family from Việt Nam to the United States at age ten through the Humanitarian Operation Program. Now residing in Seattle, she cofounded Cherry Blossom Sangha, a mindfulness community dedicated to fostering inner serenity, mutual understanding, and universal compassion.

Her diverse exploration of Buddhism, from Theravāda and Mahāyāna traditions to secular applications, has been enriched by pilgrimages to India and Nepal and a residential internship at a Zen monastery. *Budding Lotus in the West* reflects these experiences, focusing on gender equality and social change.

Nhi is also a devoted patron of Tu Viện Giác Hải, a monastery in Khánh Hòa founded by her great-uncle, the Venerable Thích Viên Giác. She holds a master's in public administration from Seattle University and enjoys exploring culinary delights from around the globe, always with a side of sriracha or chili pepper.

Nhi is represented by literary agent Leticia Gomez of Savvy Literacy. To connect with Nhi, visit www.kneetran.com/ or instagram.com/NhiYenDoTran.